Meditations of Saint Augustine

Meditations

of
Saint Augustine

with an introduction by
Jean-Clair Girard

translated by
Matthew J. O'Connell

edited by
John E. Rotelle, O.S.A.

Augustinian Press
1995

Copyright © 1995 Augustinian Heritage Institute

Cover: *Saint Augustine of Hippo*. Bartolomé
Esteban Murillo (Madrid, Musea del Prado).
Cover design: Jodi Forlizzi, Inc., Philadelphia

Library of Congress Cataloging-in-Publication Data

Augustine, Saint, Bishop of Hippo.
 [Meditationes. English]
 Meditations of Saint Augustine / with an introduction by
Jean-Clair Girard ; translated by Matthew J. O'Connell; edited
by John E. Rotelle.
 p. cm.
 Includes bibliographical references and indexes.
 ISBN 0-941491-80-3 (cloth). — ISBN 0-941491-79-X (paper)
 1. Meditations. 2. Spiritual life — Christianity — Early works
to 1800. I. Rotelle, John E. II. Title.

BR65.A89M43   1995   95-19314
242 — dc20   CIP

Augustinian Press
P.O. Box 476
Villanova, PA 19085

Contents

Foreword

The meditations presented in this book are not the work of Saint Augustine of Hippo but are truly inspired by his writings and thought. In the middle ages it was customary to copy or edit the works of great people and pen their name to the finished product. People thus thought that these works were truly the efforts of the writer named, but they were not. The name continued to be attached to the work until scientific research took place and laid out the authentic and spurious works of the early writers in the Greek and Latin traditions.

All of us are aware of the popularity of the *Imitation of Christ* right up to our own century. Before the *Imitation of Christ* it was these very *Meditations* which served as the font of spiritual nourishment for many people.

In presenting this work of the *Meditations* of Saint Augustine I recommend to the reader the introduction by Jean-Clair Giraud, which gives the historical background for each of these meditations. The introduction is also rich in its theological and liturgical presentation of these texts. I also call to mind to the reader that these meditations should be prayed or read by chapter or section. This is not a book which one reads from cover to cover.

In the Latin text, from which the English translation is derived, each meditation is divided into chapters. These chapters have been preserved in the English with the appropriate numbers. The text has been divided into sections to demonstrate that this is a meditation to be prayed rather than just read.

For the introduction, thematic guide, and notes, I am indebted to the staff of The Institute Migne in Paris for allowing me to use the work of Jean-Clair Giraud. The French translation appeared in the collection *Les Pères dans la foi,* a collection which provides integrally the major texts of the Church, and which is under the direction of A.-G. Hamman and M.-H. Congourdeau.

May you enjoy, now in English translation, what has been a bestseller for many centuries.

14 March 1995   John E. Rotelle, O.S.A.

Introduction

The *Meditations* of Saint Augustine were immensely popular during the middle ages and seem to have provided food for the prayer of many generations of Christians, and especially of many monks and nuns. They were repeatedly copied and passed from hand to hand throughout Europe down to the fifteenth century; they were sufficiently well known that soon after printing was invented they were published at Milan as early as 1475. They were reprinted in the seventeenth century by the Benedictines of Saint-Maur, whose edition can be found in volume 40 of Migne's *Patrologia Latina* (columns 901 to 942). That kind of good fortune is enough to make many writers pale with envy; the explanation is to be found essentially in the real veneration which the entire middle ages had for the name and works of Saint Augustine. This is one of the reasons for providing present-day Christians with a translation of this spiritual treasure for their meditation.

But the matter is not really as simple as I have just described it, because these *Meditations* of Saint Augustine are not by Saint Augustine. Their author has therefore been renamed Pseudo-Augustine.

Complex origins

The attribution of these meditations to Saint Augustine is not surprising; the fact is that the apocryphal texts which fervent admirers assigned to him are beyond counting. He was so imitated for centuries on end that the majority of medieval spiritual writings ended up sounding like him; André Mandouze has remarked that in that period "the Church turned Augustinian." It was an age in which the idea of literary property had not yet developed

9

and in which writers borrowed whole pages from one another's works without anyone regarding this as objectionable; the result is hundreds of quite similar texts, all of them crammed with citations that very often are identical. How then are the texts to be distinguished? The manuscripts are rarely signed and, while it is easy to recognize the major works, it is often difficult to assign to each author what belongs to him or her when a secondary text draws upon various sources, all of which claim to go back, proximately or remotely, to Saint Augustine.

This is the case with these meditations. They are sufficiently similar to what Augustine wrote that they could with some justification be assigned to him. In them are to be found citations from the Bishop of Hippo, drawn especially from the well-known *Confessions*, that suggest the meditations are from his pen. They include passages which were attributed at the time to Augustine himself. In fact one manuscript of the *Meditations* even ends with this notation: "End of the book of thoughts of Blessed Bishop Augustine, finished in 1471" (the date is obviously that of the manuscript, not of the thoughts!). There is even a story that the great Erasmus said that these meditations "were from Augustine or from someone who had read him very carefully." And it is true: in these meditations we find his outlook, the fervor of his *Confessions*, and even their rhythm and pace.

Unfortunately, a number of contradictions forces us to deny that the child is Augustine's. For example, the author says that he was baptized while in the cradle and that he was familiar with the faith from birth (see chapters 31, 39, 41). Such a claim cannot be harmonized with the long delayed and well-known conversion of the great saint. Above all, however, borrowings from Saint Gregory the Great (who came two centuries after Saint Augustine) and from the liturgy of the hours, to say nothing of borrowings from Saint Peter Damian (eleventh century), are incompatible with the authorship claimed by medieval devotion.

To whom, then, do we owe these meditations? Dom André Wilmart sheds a final light on this problem in his *Auteurs spirituels et textes dévots au Moyen Âge latin* (Paris, 1932).

Dom Wilmart's Conclusions

The main points were already known before this Benedictine scholar's work; indeed, the principal facts were already set down in the Maurist edition: the two chief authors were John, abbot of Fécamp, and Saint Anselm, philosopher and theologian, abbot of Bec-Hellouin, and archbishop of Canterbury, or, rather, a "Pseudo-Anselm," as we shall see further on. To the former the *Meditations* owe twenty-four chapters, which make up a work, the *Supputationes* ("Reflections"), which John of Fécamp dedicated to Empress Agnes, widow of Emperor Henry II (this work supplies chapters 12-27, 27-33, and 35-37 of the *Meditations*). To the second writer, the work owes chapters 1-10, 34, and 41, which are taken from the *Prayers* (*Orationes*).

Let me try to reconstruct the probable origin of the *Meditations* in their present form. To begin with, John (990-1078), abbot of Fécamp in Normandy and a holy man, decided to send to Empress Agnes a "book based on the scriptures and citations from the Fathers, for the use of all who are devoted to the contemplative life" (from the dedication of the work, which was published by Mabillon). His purpose was clear: he intended to help the widow in her prayer, inasmuch as a widow had nothing else to do but pray for her husband. The intended readership was much wider, however, for the abbot also had in mind all contemplative religious, with whose way of life he was quite familiar. His method is a traditional one: he loves to base his thoughts on the scriptures, which he cites abundantly, after the manner of Saint Augustine, and on the Fathers, his predecessors, especially Saint Augustine himself, Saint Gregory the Great, and Alcuin in the Carolingian period. His work has seven parts (these are indicated in the notes to the *Meditations*), which are preceded by some of the psalms that are developed in the parts of the work; the work thus becomes a kind of florilegium or anthology (John calls it a *defloratio* or "plucking of flowers") of all that is best calculated to serve as a guide for Christian meditation.

Note should be taken here of the many passages in the *Meditations* that are to be found in the *Mirror* (*Speculum*) of Saint Augustine and the *Confession of Faith* (*Confessio fidei*) of Alcuin, both of which were long thought to have been the source of the *Meditations*. But, if we are to believe Dom Wilmart, these two works are in fact two parts of a single work of John of Fécamp! Thus John was not drawing on the *Mirror* and the *Confession of Faith*, but simply reusing passages from his own book of reflections, the *Supputationes*, in these later texts. He does this at times in so free a manner that the result is less properly a citation than a new expression of the same idea. This hypothesis has the merit of highlighting the unitary character and, in the final analysis, the simplicity of John's work. More recently, Jean Leclercq discovered and published another source used by John, namely, his own *Theological Confession* (*Confessio theologica*).

Anselm of Bec was a neighbor of John; he obviously belonged to a younger generation, but he was quite familiar with John's work. When John's *Supputationes* became widely known, Anselm made use of them and valued them, as others did. Consequently, it is not surprising to find these two names connected with a single work. But the matter is not that simple, since the various elements of the present *Meditations* that are attributed to Anselm are in fact of varying origin. The *Prayers* of Anselm are apocryphal and made up of pieces taken from various writers of various periods. For example, it was zealous compilers of the fourteenth century who composed *Prayers* 16, 17, 18, and 19 of "Anselm" out of chapters 35-37 of John of Fécamp. That explains why we find the material in both collections. On the other hand, the attribution to John is certainly valid, for there is a clear difference of tone between the work of the two abbots. John is full of enthusiasm and gratitude, while "Anselm" is often more distressed and anguished; the three chapters in question seem to reflect more the first of these two spirits.

As for the other chapters of the *Meditations* that are attributed to Anselm, they are not to be found in John's work. Where did they come from? According to Dom Wilmart, there was a series of subsequent additions (the number of chapters is not the same in all the manuscripts), the final hand being that of an Italian Augustinian religious of the fifteenth century, to whom, in his opinion, we owe the definitive version. In the process, the original short work of John of Fécamp was augmented by a number of other texts: the present chapters 1-6 are extracts from Anselm's *Proslogion*, chapters 8-9 are a compilation from a *De spiritu et anima* of the twelfth century, which in turn is based on two works of Hugh of Saint Victor (who died in 1141); these various texts are designated in the notes of the present volume by their "official" name, that is, *Prayers* of Anselm. Also added was the eighth Prayer from the *De divina contemplatione* of John of Fécamp (= chapter 38), and a poem addressed to the Blessed Trinity and attributed to Saint Peter Damian (chapter 26). The situation in chapters 39 and 40 is less clear, since they are paraphrases rather than citations; chapter 39 could be from Saint Anselm and chapter 40 from John, but it is more likely that the later Italian compilers composed the two chapters with extracts from the two abbots. So, too, the present chapter 34, which is attributed to Anselm, seems in fact to be an anonymous text added in the fourteenth century.

All things considered, the *Meditations* as we have them may seem a heterogeneous collection, and yet the end result of the lengthy process of composition does not lack a cohesiveness that is due at once to the subject, to the authors who are combined (or to their imitators), and to the harmonization imposed on the texts. John, Peter Damian, and Anselm were all of Italian origin and all three lived in the eleventh century; the compilers who worked in ensuing centuries were careful to respect their style.

Thus we are far removed now from Saint Augustine, even though he lives on in these *Meditations* that are so steeped in his spirit. But it may be a help in saying something here about the real (or supposed) authors of the work.

John of Fécamp (990-1078)

John is the less well known of the two men, but he is at the heart of the work. He was born near Ravenna in about 990, into circles that were well educated and heavily involved in the monastic reform that was to bring such a great renewal to the Church in the eleventh and twelfth centuries. His uncle, William of Volpiano, took him along when he went to found the monastery of Saint-Bénigne in Dijon, where John made his studies and where he gave himself the sobriquet of "Little John." In 1017 John's reputation for piety led to his appointment as prior of the monastery of the Trinity in Fécamp, where he became abbot in 1028. Himself strongly drawn to contemplation, he set about enkindling fervor in his own monastery, and he undertook the reform (that is, the restoration of order) of a number of abbeys in Normandy and elsewhere. The *Meditations* are one of the means which Little John used in order to spread the spirit of prayer.

John was also called upon to settle all sorts of questions, disagreements, and even conflicts between individuals, monasteries, and kings. This role caused him many difficulties and necessitated a great deal of traveling throughout Europe, much to his dislike. He suffered a great deal from being thus torn between intense activity and his need for contemplation. He even made a pilgrimage to the Holy Land, where he was supposedly taken prisoner by the Saracens (see chapter 40, note 4). He died at Fécamp in 1078, "full of years and merits." We have various works from his pen; the most important is his little book of meditations in which "he speaks to God about God, under the inspiration of God" (J. Leclercq).

Peter Damian (1007-1072) and Anselm (1033-1109)

Saint Peter Damian was born in Ravenna, as John of Fécamp had been, but in 1007, and soon sought the eremitical life. His holiness caused popes to seek his help, and he took an active part in the great monastic reform by means of his books and his influence. He became bishop of Ostia and a cardinal, but he preferred the life of a hermit. He died in 1072, leaving various treatises on theology and a good many hymns or prayers, one of which forms chapter 26 of the *Meditations*. Evidently, his life was not unrelated to that of John of Fécamp.

Saint Anselm was born at Aosta in 1033. Initially abbot of Bec-Hellouin in Normandy, he had the opportunity to become well acquainted with John of Fécamp before the latter's death. Later on, as archbishop of Canterbury, he gave energetic leadership to the reform of the Church in England, an activity that involved quarrels with rulers. He is known above all, however, as a philosopher and a theologian, even winning the title of "the new Augustine." He is the real originator of the great philosophical movement out of which scholasticism emerged. He died at Canterbury in 1109.

The Meditations

As was pointed out above, there is a rather clear difference in tone between John and Pseudo-Anselm. The chapters from John's pen plunge us into contemplation of the mysteries of God and the action of the grace which we owe to his saving goodness. The chapters taken from Pseudo-Anselm belong to a different genre, that of prayers in which sinners beg for the grace which they greatly fear they lack. Thus John comes across to us as more serene, "Anselm" as more subject to inner turbulence.

And yet, while the two writers do not see things in the same way, they do deal with the same subject. Both are haunted by the insurmountable distance between God's world and our world here below. "God" means the Trinity with its supreme perfections; many pages are devoted to this subject, for it is a key part of the Christian faith. It is impossible fully to clarify the meaning of this mystery that has given rise to so many questions in the history of the Church, and the *Meditations* give us a sense that the question is a burning one indeed. "God" also means the invisible world, the heavenly Jerusalem, the communion of saints, in all of which we will share only when we are delivered from our present bodies. God is wholly "sweetness" (*dulcedo*), says John. Human beings, on the other hand, are exiles in a wretched land, assailed by temptations, crushed by their sins: exile, pilgrimage, tribulation are our lot.

And yet humanity has a hope, and that hope is Christ, who, because of his double nature as true human being and true God, is a bridge between human wretchedness and the divine splendor. The two writers constantly use paradoxes to speak of redemption, as they move back and forth between savior and sinners, creator and creatures, victim and the guilty (see, for example, chapters 6,

15, and 29). The Good Shepherd is always there to bring back the lost sheep (see chapter 8).

A special role is assigned to the gift of tears, which is the final recourse of sinners: by means of tears the Holy Spirit cleanses the heart and renders it receptive to the Savior's action. This is why one particular statement from the psalms is so often repeated in the *Meditations*: *My tears have been my bread day and night* (Ps 41:4). In Augustine's thinking this psalm describes the search for God. (There are a great many citations from the psalms in the *Meditations*.)

The readers of this work thus accompany the monk on his quest for the kingdom of God. With him they scan the scriptures (see the references to the monastic life in chapters 22, 25, 29, and 36) and keep their eyes fixed on the person of Christ, who is the focus of meditation (see, for example, chapters 15, 16, and 40). In the movement of the *Meditations*, however, no clear plan is to be expected; we simply move from chapter to chapter.

Alert readers will have no difficulty in realizing the extent to which the *Meditations* are permeated by the liturgy. Verbatim citations indeed are few, but echoes are frequently heard, as well as direct allusions to the *Sanctus* and the *Te Deum*.

A Thought and a Style

Does all this mean that the text has not been composed with any great care? There is, of course, an element of spontaneity in a "meditation"; that is the nature of the genre, for in it the soul allows itself to be led on by the Holy Spirit, without following a set plan. On the other hand, readers quickly perceive how carefully the phrases are shaped, perhaps too much so for our modern taste. But could it be otherwise in a work so rich in biblical and patristic references? Some of these references have been indicated in parentheses or in notes, but it must be realized that the entire text is a tissue of citations very skillfully woven together. This kind of composition can obviously not be the fruit of sheer spontaneity. We need to consider, for example, the care with which John of Fécamp handles his transitions (chapter 13). He even cites popular verses of his day (chapter 18), multiplies images in order to find the most eloquent ones (chapter 24), and strives to move the reader deeply in his descriptions of the human condition or the passion of Christ (chapters 6, 8, and 21). All this is in continuity with earlier Christian literature, which had made eager use of expressive devices ever since Augustine or even Tertullian (in chapter 2 we find one of Tertullian's favorite images: the refreshing coolness of virtue, in contrast to the searing flames of vice).

Our contemporary spirituality lays a heavy emphasis on restraint, so that we may sometimes feel a certain uneasiness as we read the *Meditations*. The linking of a series of phrases by systematically turning the noun of one into the adjective of the next (see chapters 1, 10, 17, 37) may seem artificial to us. The parallelisms and symmetries inherited from Saint Augustine (an element in his "Africanism"), the very frequent plays on words (see chapters 5 and 41), the endless lists (chapters 1, 9, 12, 18, and 29) may at times seem overdone. And yet all these are methods of developing a meditation, for it is by pondering words that we assimilate the mystery they conceal (see, for example, chapter 7). The sacred scriptures are sacred texts, and Christ, the Son of God, is the Word of God: the middle ages were always keenly conscious of these facts and set about scrutinizing words in the hope of catching in them a reflection of the Word of God.

If, then, I can offer readers any advice, it is this: they should approach the *Meditations* in the spirit of their author and look for that which they meant to convey. It would be useless (and perhaps tedious) to read them as treatises, for they are not treatises. It is necessary to meditate on them, to weigh each word and phrase in a prayer, and step by step to accept the little corner of the mystery which one or other expression may unveil for us. When they are thus read and brought to life again, they may prove to be a bedside book that will come alive in our hearts and be able to lead us into contemplation.

Conclusion

Let me go back to where I began, to the history of these *Meditations*. They were not a mere literary success; rather they enabled entire generations to make progress in God's sight. A fervent abbot back in the eleventh century condensed into one small book the finest meditations he had encountered in his reading; they served him for his prayer, and he passed them to others as a stimulus for their piety; whole monasteries drew life from this serene contemplation. Saint Anselm was drawn to them, made them his own, and nourished himself on them; even those around Saint Bernard drew upon them. People used them for their prayer from the thirteenth century down to the nineteenth, and the mystical current to which the book bears witness has continued down to our own day throughout Europe.

Who can fail to hear the accents of a Bérulle in this Christ-centered adoration. (Is not chapter 15, for example, an anticipation, five centuries earlier, of the well known Berullean "O"?) Grignion de Montfort is anticipated in the complete abandonment preached in some chapters (see chapter 40), while chapter 12 anticipates by eight centuries the famous prayer of Elizabeth of the Trinity: "O my God, Trinity whom I adore, help me to forget myself completely that I may be grounded in you, in immovable peace, as if my soul were already in eternity."

Let us in our turn enter into the communion of all those who, learning from Saint Augustine, have sought God with the help of these *Meditations*, which for centuries ranked as one of the two most widely read books, the other being the *Imitation of Christ*.

Jean-Clair Girard

1

Prayer to God for Conversion[1]

ord, my God, grant that my heart may desire you and that when it desires you it may also seek you; that when it seeks you it may also find you; that when it finds you, it may love you and by this love make up for my sins and sin no more.

Give to my heart, Lord, my God, the spirit of penance: to my soul, repentance; to my eyes, a fountain of tears; and to my hands, generosity in almsgiving.

My King, extinguish in me the desires of the flesh and light in me the fire of your love.

My Redeemer, expel from me the spirit of pride and by your grace grant me the treasure of your humility.

My Savior, remove far from me the storms of anger and in your goodness let there remain in me your patience and serenity.

My Creator, root out of me every kind of resentment and fill me with the sweetness of a gentle mind.

Grant me, most merciful Father, an unshakable faith, a hope no less strong, and a ceaseless love.

My Guide, remove from me all vanity, the inconstant mind, the straying heart, the scurrilous tongue, the haughty eye, the greedy belly. Keep me from insulting my neighbors and from harming their good name. Free me from the itch of curiosity, from the lust for wealth, from snatching at power and the desire for empty glory, from the sickness of hypocrisy and the poison of flattery, from contempt for the helpless and oppression of the weak, from the fire of avarice, the corrosion of envy, and the death of blasphemy.

Cut out of me, my Maker, all rashness, stubbornness, restlessness, idleness, torpidity, laziness, all dullness of mind and blindness of heart and obstinacy in opinion, all aggressive behavior, disobedience to the good, rejection of advice, and the unbridled tongue. Let me not prey upon the poor or do violence to the powerless or calumniate the innocent.

Do not allow me to neglect those under me or be harsh to servants or lack due regard for relatives or be hard on my neighbors.

My God, my Mercy, I beg you through your beloved Son: enable me to do the works of mercy and fulfill the obligations of piety: to be compassionate to the afflicted, to help the needy, succor the wretched, counsel the straying, console the sorrowful, raise up the oppressed, give new heart to the poor and strength to those who weep; to forgive my debtors, spare those who offend me, and love those who hate me.

Teach me to return good for evil and to despise no one but to honor all; to imitate the good and avoid the wicked, to embrace the virtues and reject the vices, to be patient in adversity and restrained in prosperity, to *set a watch over my mouth and a door in front of my lips* (Ps 141:3), to spurn under foot the things of earth and thirst for those of heaven.

2

The Sinner before God's Mercy[2]

y Maker, I have asked you for much, though
I deserve not even a little. I admit, alas, not
only that what I ask is not a gift due me, but
also that what I really deserve are punishments numerous and severe. And yet I take
courage from the tax collectors, the prostitutes, and the
thieves who have been snatched in an instant from the
jaws of the enemy and taken to the shepherd's breast.

For you, O God, Maker of all, though wonderful in all
your works, are more wonderful still for your heartfelt
mercy. Therefore you said of yourself through one of
your servants: *His tender mercies are upon all his works* (Ps
145:9). And we trust that when you spoke these words of
your whole people you meant them of each individual:
But my mercy I will not take away from him (Ps 89:34).

For you despise no one, you reject no one, you recoil
from no one except the madman who has rejected you.
That is why you do not grow angry and strike, but you
even grant your gifts to those who anger you, if they ask
for them.

My God, Horn of my salvation, and my Support,[3] to my
sorrow I have offended you and done evil before you; I
have provoked your wrath and deserved your anger. I
have sinned, and you have put up with it; I have committed offenses, and you still keep me in being. If I repent,
you spare me; if I return, you accept me; and if I put off
my return, you wait for me. You call me back when I stray

and invite me when I reject you; you rouse me when I fall asleep and embrace me when I return; you instruct me in my ignorance and give me relief in my sorrow; you snatch me from destruction and renew me after a fall; you give your gifts when I ask, are found when I seek, and open the door when I knock.[4]

Lord, God of my salvation, I know not what answer to give, what reply to make; I see no refuge, no place to hide from you. You have shown me the way of the good life, you have given me knowledge of how to walk it; you have threatened me with hell and promised me the glory of paradise. Now, *Father of mercies and God of all consolation* (2 Cor 1:3), *pierce my flesh with fear of you* (Ps 119:120) so that by fearing you I may escape what you threaten; and in your good will toward me *restore to me the joy of your salvation* (Ps 51:14) so that by loving you I may obtain what you promise.

Lord, my Strength, my Support, my God, my Refuge, and my Deliverer, tell me what I should think about you, teach me the words with which to call to you, grant me the works with which to please you. Indeed I know full well one thing that pleases you and another that you cannot refuse, for an afflicted spirit is the sacrifice you desire, and a contrite and humbled heart you accept.[5]

My God, my Helper, enrich me with these gifts, fortify me with these safeguards against the enemy, grant me this refreshing coolness against the flames of the vices, and in your fidelity open to me this refuge from passionate desires.

Lord, power that saves me, let me not be among those who believe for a while but in the time of trial fall away (Lk 8:13).[6] Overshadow my head on the day of battle;[7] be my hope on the day of affliction and my salvation in the time of tribulation.[8]

3

The Sinner's Lament before the Silent God⁹

od, my Light and my Salvation (Ps 27:1),[10] I have asked you for what I need and told you what I fear; but my conscience nags at me and the hidden recesses of my heart reproach me, while fear undoes what love urges, anxiety undermines what zeal suggests. My past life rouses fear, but your faithfulness stirs confidence; your goodness urges me on, while my own wickedness holds me back.

To be honest, the images of my vices invade my memory and shake the boldness of my presumptuous soul. For when persons deserve only hatred, how can they boldly ask for grace? When they merit punishment, how can they be rash enough to ask for glory? Those who fail to make reparation for their sins and yet seek rewards only defy the judge. Those who deserve punishment and yet demand a wage not due them insult the king, and foolish is the child who enrages a father's loving heart by sinning and then claiming a heavenly inheritance before doing penance.

Father, what deeds have I to remember? I deserved death but I ask for life. I have angered my King, and yet I now shamelessly ask his protection. I have shown contempt for the Judge but now demand that he be my helper. I have arrogantly refused to listen to my Father and yet I now presume that he will be my protector. Alas, how late I have come to myself, and how slowly I hasten!

Only after being wounded do I try to run, though when I was still healthy I disdained to avoid the missiles thrown at me. I neglected to look ahead to threats, and now I am open to imminent death. I have inflicted wound upon wound because I did not fear to add sin to sin. I have applied a new source of corruption to my scars by adding new sins to the old, while my mad itch to offend has undone what divine medicine had knit together. The skin that had grown over the wounds and hidden my disease decayed as the underlying corruption broke forth again and my repeated sins rendered vain the forgiveness I had received.[11] I knew indeed that it is written: *On the day the just man sins all the good works he has done will be forgotten* (Ez 18:24). If, then, the past good works of a just person are rendered vain when he falls, how much more the repentance of a sinner who returns to his ways? How often I have returned to my sins like a dog to its vomit[12] and a pig to its wallow![13]

It is impossible for me to confess — because it is impossible for me to remember — how many ignorant persons I have taught to sin, how many I have persuaded to sin against their will, how many I have forced to sin when they resisted, with how many I went along as they willingly fell. For how many have I not laid snares as they went or opened up a pit on their way, and then did not fear to forget what I had not shrunk from doing![14]

But you, just Judge, have counted all these things up like money in a sack; you noted all the paths I traveled and counted all my steps. You remained silent and said nothing. Woe is me, now that you cry out at last like a woman in labor.[15]

4

Fear of the Judge[16]

ord, God of gods, who are exalted far above all wickedness, I know that you will come openly and not be forever silent, *when a fire flames up before you and a mighty storm rages around you, on the day when you call the heavens down and the earth to pass judgment on your people.*[17] Then all my sins will be laid bare before countless people, and all my iniquities will be made known to the hosts of angels: not only my deeds but my thoughts and words.

I shall stand helpless before my judges, all those who have outstripped me in good works; I shall be dismayed by my accusers, all those who have given me the example of a good life; I shall be convicted by the witnesses, all those who admonished me with helpful words and offered themselves as models with their holy actions.

My Lord, I have nothing to say, no answer to give. And as if I were already facing that critical moment, my conscience torments me, and I am tortured by the secrets of my heart: the greed that straitens me, the pride that accuses me, the envy that consumes me, the lust that inflames me, the licentiousness that distresses me, the gluttony that shames me, the drunkenness that abashes me, the malicious gossip that tears at others, the ambition that causes them to stumble, the rapacity that strikes at them, the discord that scatters them, the anger that agitates them, the inconstancy that disappoints them, the laziness that makes me a burden to them, the hypocrisy that deceives them, the flattery that leads them to shipwreck, the favoritism that puffs them up, the calumny that destroys their peace.[18]

My Deliverer from a wrathful people, see who it is with whom I have lived from the day of my birth, for whom I have been zealous, with whom I have kept faith. The dearest objects of my devotion have condemned me; those I praised have criticized me: the friends on whom I relied, the teachers I obeyed, the masters I served, the advisers whom I trusted, the fellow citizens with whom I lived, the members of my household, whose outlook I shared.

Woe is me, my King and my God, *that my sojourning is prolonged!* Woe is me, my Enlightener, for *I have dwelt with the inhabitants of Kedar*. And when the holy man speaks of his sojourn as *long*, with how much greater right can I, an unhappy man, say that *my soul has been* too long *a sojourner* (Ps 120:5)?[19]

God, my Support, no living thing will be justified in your sight.

My Hope, there is no human being that you can find just if you judge him without exercising your mercy. Unless you take the first step by having mercy on the wicked, there will be no one for you to glorify as just.

For, my Salvation, I believe what I have heard: that *it is your generous kindness that leads* me *to repentance* (Rom 2:4). It is you, my *strong tower* (Ps 62:3), whose honeyed lips have said: *None can come to me unless the Father who sent me draws them* (Jn 6:44).

Indeed, it is because you have instructed me and so mercifully formed me that with all my heart and all the force of my mind I call upon you, almighty Father, together with your beloved Son and upon you, his sweet Child, together with his Spirit of peace: *draw me, that I may delight to run after you and the perfume of your ointments* (Sg 1:3).

5

Prayer to the Father through the Son[20]

 call upon you, my God, I call upon you for you are near to all who call upon you, provided they call upon you in truth.[21] But you are Truth itself; in your mercy, therefore, teach me to call upon you in you, O holy Truth.

I have no idea of how to set about this, but I plead with you to teach me, O blessed Truth. For to know apart from you is to waste my efforts, whereas to know you is to know what is complete and perfect.

Instruct me, divine Wisdom, and teach me your law. I firmly believe that those whom you instruct and whom you teach your law are blessed. I desire to call upon you and desire to do so in truth, But what does it mean to call upon the Truth in truth but to call upon the Father in the Son?[22]

Yes, holy Father, your word is truth, and truth is the source of all your words. And the source of your words is the Word who was in the beginning.[23]

In this source I adore you, the supreme Source.

In this Word of truth I call upon you, O perfect Truth, that you may guide me to that same truth and teach it to me.[24]

What could be more delightful than to call upon the Begetter in the name of his Only-begotten, to sway the Father to mercy by reminding him of his Son, to soften the King's heart by naming his offspring to him? Thus the guilty are often rescued from prison, slaves are freed from their chains, and those sternly sentenced to death not only recover their lives but even have extraordinary favors shown them, all because these unfortunates let angry princes know the pity shown them by their beloved sons; thus, too, misbehaving servants avoid punishment from their masters when indulgent sons intercede for them.

In like manner, almighty Father, I appeal to you in the name of the love of your almighty Son: *bring my soul out of prison that it may praise your name* (Ps 142:8); I beg you in the name of your coeternal only Son, free me from the chains of sin; be appeased and through the intercession of your beloved Son who sits at your right hand restore me to life even though my own merits threaten me with the sentence of death.

For I know not what other intercessor with you I may obtain, save him who is *the propitiation for our sins* (1 Jn 2:2), *who sits at your right hand and intercedes for us.*[25]

See, he is my advocate with you, God and Father!

He is the high priest who does not need the blood of another to make expiation because he is covered with his own radiant blood.

He is the holy victim, pleasing and perfect, offered and accepted in an odor of sweetness.

He is the spotless Lamb who was silent before his shearers[26] and who did not open his mouth when he was slapped and spat upon and insulted.

He is the one who committed no sin and yet bore my sins and healed my wounds with his own bruises.[27]

6

The Father Is Reminded
of the Son's Suffering[28]

oly Father, look upon your most holy Son and the unholy things he suffered for me. Most merciful King, look upon the one who suffers, and remember with lenience the one for whom he suffered. Is he not innocent, the Son whom you handed over to redeem a slave? Is it not the author of life who was *led like a sheep to slaughter* (Is 53:7) and, *becoming obedient even unto death* (Phil 2:8), did not hesitate to undergo the cruelest kind of death?

Recall, O Arranger of all salvation, that this is the one who, though begotten out of your perfection, desired to share my weakness. Yes, it is your very godhead that put on my nature and mounted the gallows of the cross, and that endured harsh torment in the nature it had assumed.

Lord, my God, turn your majestic gaze to this work of ineffable goodness. Look upon your dear Son with his body stretched out on the cross; see the innocent hands streaming with holy blood; and, being appeased, forgive the sins which my hands have committed. See the helpless side pierced by a cruel lance, and renew me in the holy fountain which I believe flowed from it. See the spotless feet that never *stood in the way of sinners* (Ps 1:1) but always walked according to your law, and are now transfixed by frightful nails; then make me walk in your paths and, in your kindness, compel me to hate all the ways of wickedness.

Merciful One, turn me away from the way of wickedness; show me your favor and make me choose the way of truth.

King of the saints, I pray you by this Holy of holies, this Redeemer of mine, to make me run in the way of your commandments so that I may be able to be united in spirit with him who did not shrink from putting on my human nature.

Do you not see, loving Father, how the young head of your dear Son bends on his snowy neck as it relaxes in a most precious death?

Most merciful Creator, look upon the humanity of your beloved Son, and take pity on the weakness of your frail creature. His bared breast is gleaming white, his side is red with blood, his contracted organs are withered, his beautiful eyes are dimmed, his royal lips are pale, his extended arms are stiff, his legs hang down like pieces of marble, the flood of holy blood bathes his pierced feet.

Look, glorious Father, at the torn limbs of your dear Son, and remember with pity of what stuff I am made. Look upon the sufferings of the God-man and lift from its wretched state the human race that you have created. See the torments of the Redeemer and forgive the sins of those he has redeemed.

My Lord, it is he whom you have struck because of your people's sins, even though he is the beloved one in whom you were well pleased.[29] He is the innocent one in whom there was no deceit, and yet you counted him among the wicked.[30]

7

God's Wonderful Plan
in the Sufferings of Christ[31]

hat have you done, dear Child, to be judged in this way? What have you done, young man who are so alive, that you should be thus mistreated? What is your crime? What harm have you done? Why this death, this condemnation? Ah, it is I who delivered the wounding blow; it is I who bear the guilt of your death. I inflicted the bruises you suffered and the torments you bore. I was responsible for your death, mine was the sin for which you suffered. What a wonderful covenant was at work in this severity! What an ineffable plan was being carried out in this mystery! The wicked sin, and the just man is punished; the guilty are at fault, and the innocent one suffers blows; the evil offend, and the faithful one is condemned; what the wicked deserve, the good man suffers; the servant does wrong and the master pays the penalty; human beings sin and God endures the consequences.

Into what depths, Son of God, did your humility take you? How hot did your love burn? How far did your fidelity and goodness go? How far did your love and compassion reach?

I acted sinfully, you suffered the penalty; I committed the crime, you paid the price; I did evil, you were subjected to torment; I exalted myself in pride, you humbled yourself; I was inflamed with passion, you were straitened; I was disobedient, you paid for my disobedience with your obedience; I yielded to gluttony, you went hungry; desire led me to the forbidden fruit of the tree, perfect love led you to the cross; I dared what was forbidden, you suffered the rack; I take delight in food, you struggle on the gibbet; I indulge in pleasures, you are torn by nails; I taste the savory fruit, you the bitterness of gall; laughing Eve rejoices with me, weeping Mary suffers with you.[32]

See, King of glory, see how great is my wickedness and how resplendent your love! See how evident is my lack of holiness and how shining your holiness!

My King and my God, what return shall I make to you for all that you have given to me? Nothing in the human heart can match such rewards. Can human wisdom devise anything comparable to the divine compassion? It is not in the creature's power to do anything that can adequately repay the Creator for his protection.

But in this wonderful plan of yours, O Son of God, there is a part my weakness can play, provided that my soul is deeply moved by your visitation and crucifies the flesh with its vices and lusts;[33] for if you grant it this favor, it already begins as it were to suffer with you the death you deigned to die for sin.[34] Thus through the interior victory it wins under your leadership, it will be armed to gain the external trophy, for to the extent that it conquers spiritual persecution, it will not fear, in its love for you, being put to the material sword. Thus if the littleness it owes to its natural condition is able to please you in your goodness, it will be able, in its own limited way, to match the greatness of its Creator.

This heavenly medicine, good Jesus, is the antidote provided by your love. I pray you by your mercies that are from old to pour this medicine into my wounds; let it expel the poison of the serpent's bite and restore me to the health that was in the beginning; let me taste the nectar of your sweetness and be able with all my heart to scorn the seductive triumphs of the world and for your sake fear none of its adversities; let me be mindful of my lasting nobility and treat with disdain the winds of the world's passing excitements.

Let me find nothing sweet apart from you, nothing pleasing, nothing of value, nothing beautiful save you. Let all things be worthless in my eyes, all things squalid, apart from you.

Let what is contrary to you be offensive to me as well, and let my ceaseless desire be for what pleases you.

Let any joy apart from you be wearisome to me, and let me find my joy in sorrow for your sake.

Let your name revive me, the remembrance of you console me; let my tears be my food[35] as day and night I seek your salvation, and let the law of your mouth be my happiness more than treasures of gold and silver.[36]

Let me love to obey you and shrink from resisting you.

My Hope, I appeal to your omnipotence to forgive my sins. Open my ears to your commandments and do not allow my heart — I appeal to your holy Name! — to yield to the solicitations of wickedness so that I end up excusing my sins.

I beg you also, by your holy humility, let pride not come upon me nor the hand of the sinner touch me.

8

The Passion of Christ Brings the Father's Forgiveness[37]

lmighty God, Father of my Lord, decide now in your goodness how you will show me mercy, for the most precious thing I have I have devoutly offered to you, the dearest thing I have I have humbly presented to you.

I have kept nothing for myself that I have not set before your Majesty; I have nothing left to add, because I have placed my entire hope in you.

I have sent you my beloved Advocate, your Son; I have sent your glorious Child as mediator between you and me; I have sent him, that is, as the intercessor through whom I hope to receive pardon.

I have sent him by my words, this Word who was sent by his deeds in my behalf, and I have offered you as payment the death of your holy Son, a death which I believe he suffered on my account.

I believe that you sent him, a divine person, to assume my humanity, in which he thought it right to endure chains, blows, and being spat upon and insulted, and even to suffer the cross, the nails, and the spear. This humanity had once been shaken by the sobs of the newborn child, restrained by the swaddling clothes of infancy, troubled by the labors of young manhood, worn by fasts and vigils, wearied by journeys. Later it was struck with whips, torn by tortures, numbered among the dead, and at last endowed with the glory of the resurrection. This humanity he introduced into the joys of heaven and placed it at the right hand of your Majesty. He it is who reconciles me to you and wins your favor for me.

In your mercy look upon this Son whom you begot and this servant whom you have redeemed. Look upon the Maker and do not scorn his creature. Cheerfully embrace the Shepherd and in your mercy receive the sheep he carries on his own shoulders. He is that most faithful of shepherds, who by his many and varied labors sought the sheep that had long been wandering among the craggy hills and steep valleys, and rejoicing took upon his shoulders the sheep that was fainting and dying due to its long exile but was found at last. With an extraordinary effort of love he raised it from the depths of anarchy and in his loving embrace carried it back to the ninety-nine, this one sheep that had been lost.[38]

Lord, my God, almighty King, see how the Good Shepherd is bringing back to you that which you gave him. In accordance with your plan he undertook to save the human race and has restored it to you purified of all sin. See how your beloved Son reconciles to you your creatures that had wandered far from you. The loving Shepherd reunites to your flock the sheep which the thief had driven away with violence. He brings into your presence once again the servants whom conscience had turned into fugitives, so that those who deserved punishment win pardon instead through this defender and those who could expect hell for their sins now trust that under this great leader they may be brought back to their native land.

Holy Father, I was able to offend you by my own power, but I was unable to reconcile myself to you by my own power.

My God, your beloved Son came to my aid: he shared my humanity so that he might heal its weakness and so that the very humanity which had offended you and incurred guilt might offer you a sacrifice of praise. He thereby reconciled me to your loving self and sits now at your right hand where he shows himself for ever to be of one nature with me. He is my hope, he is my whole confidence. You may scorn me for my wickedness, as is only right, but look upon me with mercy for the sake of the love your beloved Son has shown me. See in your Son a reason to have pity on your servant. See the sacrament of his flesh and do away with the guilt of my flesh. Each time that the wounds of your beloved Son open before you, let my sins, I pray you, vanish from before you. Each time that the precious blood from his sacred side gleams before you, let the corruption that stains me, I pray you, be washed away.

And since it is the flesh that roused you to anger, let the flesh incline you to mercy, so that, as the flesh led me into sin, so the flesh may bring me forgiveness. Great is the punishment which my sinfulness deserved, but far greater is the forgiveness which the goodness of my Redeemer claims as its right. Great is my injustice, but greater still is the justice of the Redeemer.[39] For as much as God is greater than human beings, so much is my wickedness inferior to his goodness, both in quantity and in value. For what sin could a human being commit that has not been paid for by the Son of God made man? To what heights can pride raise itself that are not laid low by such great humility? What sway could death possibly have that would not be overcome by the suffering of God's Son on the cross?

My God, if the offenses of sinful human beings were weighed against the grace of the Creator who redeems them, less great would be the distance between East and West or between lowest hell and highest heaven.

Creator of the light, forgive now my sins because of the immense sufferings of your beloved Son. I beg you, let his devotion now win forgiveness for my impiety,[40] his restraint for my waywardness, his meekness for my inso-

38

lence. Let his humility be only all the greater because of my pride, his patience because of my impatience, his kindness because of my hardness of heart, his obedience because of my disobedience, his serenity because of my restlessness, his sweetness because of my bitterness, his mildness because of my anger, his love because of my cruelty.[41]

9

Invocation of the Holy Spirit[42]

Love of the divine majesty, holy exchange between the omnipotent Father and his blessed Son, almighty Spirit Paraclete, merciful consoler of the sorrowing, enter mightily into the innermost recesses of my heart and there, loving Guest, let the dark hiding-places of my neglected dwelling know the joy of your radiant light, and let your abundant dew make them fruitful after they have long been withering from aridity and neglect. Burn with your spear of love the hidden wounds of the interior self; burn its tepid heart with your salutary flames, and feed the depths of mind and body as you illumine them with the fire of your holy fervor. Let me drink from the stream of your delight[43] so that I may no longer find any pleasure in the poisoned sweetness of worldly things.

Judge me, O Lord, and distinguish my cause from the nation that is not holy (Ps 43:1); *teach me to do your will, for you are my God* (Ps 143:10).

I believe, then, that in whomever you make your dwelling, there you also build a house for the Father and the Son. Blessed are they who have you as their guest, because through you the Father and the Son will also make their dwelling in them.[44]

Come now, come, most kind Consoler of the sorrowing soul and its Helper in good times and in trials.[45]

Come, purifier from sin and healer of wounds.

Come, strength of the weak and raiser of the fallen.

40

Come, teacher of the humble and destroyer of the proud.

Come, loving father of orphans and affectionate judge of widows.

Come, hope of the poor and restorer of the weak.

Come, star of the sailor and harbor of the shipwrecked.

Come, unmatched adornment of all the living and sole salvation of the dying.

Come, holiest of spirits, come and take pity on me: conform me to yourself and stoop to me in mercy, so that in accordance with the multitude of your mercy my littleness may win the heart of your greatness and my weakness of your strength, through Jesus Christ, my Savior, who with the Father lives and reigns in your unity through endless ages. Amen.

10

Prayer of Humble Self-Judgment[46]

know, Lord, I know and admit that I do not deserve your love for me; but you are certainly not undeserving of my love for you. I am unworthy to serve you, but you are not unworthy of your creature's service.

Grant me, then, Lord, that which makes you worthy, and I will be worthy insteady of unworthy. As you desire, make me stop sinning, so that I will be able to serve you as I ought.

Grant that I may so watch over, guide, and end my life that I may fall asleep in peace and rest in you.

Grant that at the end I may have a restful sleep, a secure rest, and eternal security. Amen.

11

Profession of Faith in the Trinity[47]

ith our whole heart and our mouth we confess, praise, and bless you, God the unbegotten Father, the only-begotten Son, and the Holy Spirit Paraclete, the holy and undivided Trinity. To you be glory through endless ages. Amen.

12

Contemplation of God's Perfections[48]

upreme Trinity, one in power and undivided in majesty, our God, God almighty, I, the least of your servants and an insignificant member of your Church, profess my faith in you. I confess my faith and I honor you with the sacrifice of praise I owe to you because of the knowledge and ability which you have deigned to bestow on me who am so little. And because I have no external gifts to offer you, I gladly and exultantly offer you, with unfeigned faith and a pure conscience, these prayers of praise which I find within me due to your merciful generosity.[49]

King of heaven and Lord of earth, I believe with all my heart and confess with my mouth that you are Father and Son and Holy Spirit, three in persons and one in substance, true God almighty, whose nature is one, simple, incorporeal, invisible, and unlimited.

"Everything in you is equally perfect and perfectly equal. You are great without quantity, good without quality, everlasting without time, life without death, strength without weakness, truth without falsehood. Your whole being is everywhere without location in space, you are present everywhere without confinement to place, you fill everything though you are not extended, you are to be found everywhere without limiting yourself, you transcend everything without need of movement, you dwell within everything without being restricted to anything. You create everything though you have no need of it, you

43

govern everything without effort, you give all things their beginning though you have no beginning, you make all mutable things though you are immutable."[50]

You are infinitely great, unlimited in power, supremely good and incomprehensibly wise, awesome in your counsels, just in your judgments, unfathomable in your thoughts, true in all you say, holy in all your works, and abounding in mercy. You are patient with sinners and merciful to the repentant. You are ever the same, eternal and everlasting, immortal and changeless. Space does not extend you nor narrow place constrict you nor any vessel hem you in.

No will influences you, no necessity compels you to change. No sorrows trouble you, no joys soothe you. Forgetfulness takes nothing from you nor does remembrance restore anything to you; past things do not pass away from you nor things future come to you. No source gave you your beginning, time brings you no increase, nor shall any chance put an end to you.

You live eternally before the ages, in the ages, and for the ages. Unending praise and everlasting glory are yours, supreme power and unmatched honor, an eternal reign and power unending, through infinite and unwearying and immortal ages. Amen.

13

The Mystery of the Incarnation Strengthens Our Hope

lmighty Trinity and only God, you who search hearts and probe them, I have thus far proclaimed your omnipotent majesty and majestic omnipotence. I now confess before you for my salvation what I believe in my heart for my justification: how at the end of the ages you deigned to come to the help of the human race.

Nowhere, Father God, do we read of you that you were sent, but of your Son the apostle says: *When the fullness of time came, God sent his Son* (Gal 4:4). When he says *sent*, he makes it clear that the Son was sent into this world and came when he was born of Blessed Mary ever virgin and appeared in the flesh as a true and complete human being. But what does the greatest of the evangelists say of him? *He was in the world, and the world was made by him* (Jn 1:10). Thus he was sent by means of his humanity to where he always was and is in his divinity. I believe with all my heart and confess with my mouth that this sending was the work of the entire Trinity.[51]

How you loved us, holy and good Father! How you loved us, faithful Creator, who did not spare even your own Son but handed him over to the wicked for our sake! He was obedient to you unto death, *even unto death on a cross* (Phil 2:8), as he took the decree of our sins and nailed it to the cross,[52] thus crucifying sin and slaying death. He alone was *free among the dead* (Ps 88:6), for he had the power to lay down his life and take it up again.[53] For us he became before you both victor and victim, and indeed victor because victim. For our sake he became before you both priest and sacrifice, and indeed priest because sacrifice.[54]

Rightly, then, is my strong hope set upon him, for you will heal all my weaknesses through him who sits at your right hand and makes intercession for us.[55]

My weaknesses, Lord, are great and numerous, numerous and great. I know and confess that the prince of this world has many a hold on me, but I beg of you: deliver me through him who sits at your right hand, our Redeemer in whom that prince found nothing belonging to him.

Justify me through him *who committed no sin and in whose mouth there was no guile* (Is 53:9; 1 Pt 2:22). Through our head, who is without stain, free one who is but a lowly and weak member.[56] I entreat you, deliver me from my sins, my vices, my falsenesses, my negligences. Fill me with your holy perfections and strengthen me in the ways of goodness. Grant that for the sake of your holy name I may persevere in the good works you desire and be faithful to your will until the end.

14

Thanksgiving for the Gifts of the Savior

might have despaired at my many, many sins and my infinite negligences, unless your Word, O God, had become flesh and dwelt among us. But I no longer dare to despair, for when we were enemies, we were reconciled by the death of your Son; how much more then have we now been saved from your wrath by him?[57] All my hope and all my well-founded trust are in the precious blood which he shed for us and for our salvation. In him I breathe; trusting in him, I long to reach you, not by any justice of my own but by the justice which resides in your Son, our Lord Jesus Christ.

"O God, merciful and kind lover of humankind, who when we did not exist exerted your power to create us through Jesus Christ your Son, our Lord, and who when we were lost by our own sin brought us back to yourself in a wonderful way! I thank you for your faithful mercy,"[58] and with all my heart I thank you over and over for the ineffable and marvelously kind love which you showed to us, who are so wretched and unworthy, by sending your only-begotten Son from your heart into our midst, that he might then save us, the children of wrath, the children of perdition.

I thank you for his holy incarnation and birth and for his glorious Mother, from whom he deigned to take flesh for our sake and for our salvation, so that he might be true

God from God and true human being from human being. I thank you for his passion and cross, his death and resurrection, his ascension into heaven, and his sitting at your right hand.

For, forty days after his resurrection, in the sight of his disciples he ascended beyond all the heavens and, as he had promised, he poured out the Holy Spirit on your adopted children.[59]

I thank you for the holy shedding of his precious blood by which we have been redeemed, and for the holy and life-giving mystery of his body and blood which we eat and drink daily in your Church, by which we are washed and sanctified, and by which we are made sharers in the one supreme divinity.

I thank you for the marvelous and ineffable love with which you loved us despite our unworthiness and saved us through your beloved only Son. For *you so loved the world that you gave your only-begotten Son, so that whoever believes in him may not perish but may have eternal life* (Jn 3:16). *This is eternal life, that we should know you, the true God, and Jesus Christ whom you sent* (Jn 17:3), with a true faith and conduct worthy of faith.

15

The Immense Love of God in the Restoration of the Human Race

 boundless love! O charity beyond compare![60] To free a slave you handed over your own Son. God became a human being so that lost humanity might be snatched from the power of the demon.

What a most generous lover of humanity is your Son, our God, who in his dedication did not regard it as enough to stoop and become a human being through the Virgin Mary but required that he undergo the torment of the cross and shed his blood for us and for our salvation! The faithful God came; he came because of his fidelity and goodness, he came to seek out and save what had been lost. He sought the lost sheep; he sought and found it and carried it back on his shoulders to the fenced-in sheepfold,[61] this faithful Lord and most tender shepherd.

O love, O fidelity! Who ever heard of such a thing? Who can fail to be stunned by a heart so full of mercy? Who will not wonder, who will not rejoice? Because of your excessive love for us, you sent your Son in the likeness of sinful flesh in order to condemn sin where sin resides, so that we might be made your just children in him.[62] "For he is the true Lamb," the spotless Lamb, "who took away the sins of the world; by dying he destroyed our death and by rising he restored our life."[63]

But what can we give back to you, our God, for so many benefits of your mercy? What praise can we offer, what thanksgiving? Even if we had the knowledge and power of the blessed angels, we could make no repayment worthy of such fidelity and love. Even if all the members of our body were turned into tongues, our littleness would be inadequate to offer you worthy praise. For beyond all understanding is the immeasurably great love you showed our unworthy selves simply because you are good and faithful. For your Son, our Lord, became not an angel but a descendant of Abraham[64] and became like us in everything but sin.

It was by thus taking a human and not an angelic nature and glorifying it with the robe of holy resurrection and immortality that he elevated it beyond all the heavens, beyond all the choirs of angels, beyond cherubim and seraphim, and placed it at your right hand. There the angels praise it and the dominations adore it, while all the powers of heaven tremble before the man-God who is set over them.[65] And in this humanity is founded all my hope and all my trust.

For in Jesus Christ our Lord resides a part of each of us, our flesh and blood. But where part of me reigns, there I believe that I too reign. And where my flesh is glorified, I recognize that I too am glorified. Where my blood rules, I see that I too rule. Although I am a sinner, I do not lose hope because there exists this grace-given communion. And if my sins bar the way, my substance requires that I be there. My sins may exclude me, but my communion in nature does not force me away. For the Lord is not so cruel as to forget humanity and not remember the creature whom he himself assumed, or not to want me for its sake after accepting it for my sake.

Indeed the Lord our God is merciful and most kind, and it is his own flesh, his own members, his own entrails that he loves in our God and Lord Jesus Christ, who is so gracious and kind and merciful. In him we have already risen from the dead, in him we have already ascended into heaven, in him we are already seated in the heavenly places. It is our flesh who loves us; in him we have the claim made by our own blood. We are truly his members and his flesh.

Finally, he is our head, on which the whole body depends, as it is written: *Bone of my bone and flesh of my flesh* and *They shall be two in one flesh* (Gn 2:23-24), and again, according to the apostle, *No man ever hates his own flesh but nourishes and loves it....This is a great mystery; I am speaking of Christ and the Church* (Eph 5:29.32).[66]

16

Prayer Inspired by the Mystery of Two Natures and One Person in Christ

ith lips and heart and all my powers I thank you, our God, Lord of infinite mercy, for all the compassionate gifts by which in wonderful ways you deigned to help us when we were lost. This you did through your Son, our Savior and Restorer, who died because of our sins and rose for our justification[67] and who now, in life unending, sits at your right hand and intercedes for us.[68]

At the same time he joins you in taking pity on us, for he is God from you, Father, and is coeternal with you and consubstantial with you in every respect, so that he is able to win for us an everlasting salvation. To him as a human being, and thus less than you, you have given *all power in heaven and on earth* (Mt 28:18), so that *at the name of Jesus every knee should bend, of those in heaven and on earth and under the earth, and every tongue should confess that the Lord Jesus Christ is in* your *glory*, O God, the almighty Father (Phil 2:10-11).

For you established him as judge of the living and the dead; you yourself judge no one, but have given all judgment over to your Son,[69] in whose bosom *are hidden all the treasures of wisdom and knowledge* (Col 2:3). He is both witness and judge: *the judge and the witness* (Jer 29:23) whose gaze no sinful conscience can evade, for *all things are naked and open to his eyes* (Heb 4:13). He who was judged unjustly will *judge the world with equity and the peoples with justice* (Ps 96:13). Therefore with all my heart I bless and glorify your holy name, almighty and merciful Lord, because of this wonderful and ineffable union of divinity and humanity in a single person, so that there is not a God and also a man, but one and the same is both God and man, man and God. But even though the Word became a human being in a marvelous act of condescension, neither of the two natures was changed into the other. There was no addition of a fourth person to the Trinity. The substance of the Word of God and the substance of the human being were not commingled; rather what was assumed from us entered into God, while that which had never been continued to be what it had always been.

O wonderful mystery! O ineffable exchange! O marvelous and always astounding goodness of the divine mercy! We were unworthy servants and, look! we have become children of God, heirs of God and coheirs with Christ.[70] How has this happened to us, and how shall we respond to it?

I ask you, most merciful God and Father, in the name of your incalculably great fidelity, goodness, and love, to make us worthy of the many great promises of this same Jesus Christ, your Son and our Lord. *Command your strength and confirm what you have wrought in us* (Ps 68:29). Complete what you have begun, so that we may be able to attain to the fullness of your gracious love. Enable us through your Holy Spirit to understand and deserve and always venerate with due honor this *great mystery of godliness, which was manifested in the flesh, was justified in the spirit, appeared to the angels, was preached to the Gentiles, has been believed in the world, and has been taken up into glory* (1 Tm 3:16).[71]

17

We Must Serve God for God's Own Sake

ow great is our debt to you, Lord our God, for having redeemed us at such a price and saved us by so great a gift and come to our aid with so glorious a blessing! How greatly we in our wretchedness should fear and love, bless and praise, honor and glorify you who thus loved us, thus saved us, thus sanctified us, and thus exalted us! To you we owe any power we exercise, any knowledge we have, any life that is in us. Who has anything that is not yours?

It is you, Lord our God, from whom every good comes; for your own sake and for the sake of your holy name grant us your blessings so that with your own gifts we may serve you and truly please you and pay you back in daily praise for so many blessings inspired by your mercy. For there is no other way than by your own gracious gift that we can serve and please you. *Every best gift and every perfect gift is from above, coming down from the Father of lights, with whom there is no change nor shadow of alteration* (Jas 1:17).

Lord our God, faithful God, gracious God, omnipotent God, "infinite and ineffable God, creator of all things and Father of our Lord Jesus Christ, you sent this beloved Son of yours and our sweet Lord from your bosom into our midst, so that he might assume our life and give us his. Thus he is perfect God from you, Father, and perfect human being from his mother: wholly God and wholly man, one and the same Christ, eternal and in time, immortal and destined to die, creator and created, strong and weak, conqueror and conquered, nourisher and nourished, pastor and sheep, dying in time and living with you eternally. He promised those who love him a place in eternal life and told us: *Whatever you ask the Father in my name, he will give to you* (Jn 15:16)."[72] I ask you in the name of this high priest and true pontiff and good shepherd who offered himself in sacrifice as he laid down his life for his sheep, and in the name of him who sits at your right hand and intercedes for us, our Redeemer and Advocate — I beg of your goodness and fidelity, O God who are the most merciful and loving and kind lover of human beings, "grant that with this same Son of yours and with your Holy Spirit I may bless and glorify you in everything, with great contrition of heart and a fountain of tears, with great reverence and awe, because where the substance is one, the gift can only be one."[73]

But because *the corruptible body weighs down the soul* (Wis 9:15), rouse my torpid mind, I pray you, and grant me to persevere energetically in your precepts and in praise of you night and day. Grant that my heart may burn within me and a fire may flame up in my meditation.[74] "And since your only-begotten Son has said that *No one comes to me unless drawn by the Father who sent me* and *No one comes to the Father except through me* (Jn 6:44; 14:6), I ask and humbly pray: draw me always to him, and let him lead me at last to where he sits at your right hand; where life is everlasting and everlastingly blessed; where perfect love exists and no fear; where there is everlasting day and all have one spirit; where there is supreme and sure security and secure tranquillity and tranquil joy and joyous happiness and happy eternity and eternal blessedness, and an unending blessed vision and praise of you; where you live and reign eternally with him and he with you in the communion of the Holy Spirit, God forever and ever. Amen."[75]

18

Prayer to Christ

hrist God, my hope, sweet lover of humanity,
Light, way, life, salvation, peace, and glory of all who are yours,
For whose salvation you willed to bear all things:
Flesh, bonds, cross, wound, death and burial.
You conquered death and after three days rose,
Were seen by your disciples and restored wavering hearts.
After forty days you ascended to the heights of heaven,
Where you live forever, ruling now and through all ages.[76]

You, my living and true God, my holy Father,[77] my faithful Lord, my great King, my good Shepherd, my sole Teacher, my helper in time of trouble, my beautiful beloved, my living Bread, my eternal Priest, my guide to the fatherland, my true Light, my holy sweetness, my right Way, my radiant Wisdom, my pure simplicity, my peaceful harmony, my secure guardian, my blessed portion, my everlasting salvation, my great mercy, my unyielding patience, my spotless Victim, my holy redemption, my hope of the future, my perfect charity, my holy resurrection, my eternal Life, my blessed joy and vision that shall never end. I pray, beg, and beseech you: let me walk by your power and come to you and rest in you who are *the way, the truth, and the life* (Jn 14:6), and apart from whom no one comes to the Father. For my desire is for you, sweet and lovely Lord.

O radiance of the Father's glory! You who sit upon the cherubim and gaze into the abyss, the true light, the light that dispels darkness, the unfailing light, *on whom the angels desire to look* (1 Pt 1:12). See, I lay my heart before you: scatter its darkness, so that it may be bathed more completely in the light of your love. "Give yourself to me, my God; restore yourself to me. I show you my love, but if it is too little, give me strength to love you more. I cannot measure its shortcomings and learn how much more I need to love you in order that my life may hasten to your embrace and never turn away from you until it is hidden in the sanctuary of your presence.[78] All I know is this, that unless you are with me, and not only beside me but in my very self, for me there is nothing but evil, and whatever riches I have, unless they are my God, they are only poverty."[79]

For you alone are the good that cannot change to something better or grow less, since you alone simply are and in you there is no difference between living and living in blessedness, for you are your own blessedness. But your creatures, for whom living and living happily are not identical, owe it to your grace alone both that they live and that they live happily. Therefore we need you, but you do not need us, for even if we did not exist at all, there would be no lessening of the good which you are in yourself. Consequently, we must always cling to you, our Lord, in order that by the continuous help of your grace we may be able to live holy, devout, and upright lives. At times indeed we are pulled downward by the weight of our weakness; but then we are set on fire by your gift and carried upward; we burn and we go forward; we ascend in our hearts and we sing a song of ascents.[80]

It is with your fire, the fire of your goodness, that we burn and go forward. To what do we ascend? To the peace of Jerusalem, for *I rejoiced at what was said to me: we shall go into the house of the Lord* (Ps 122:1). Your good will toward us has placed us there, and we desire naught else but to remain there forever.

But *while we are in the body, we are absent from* you, O Lord (2 Cor 5:6); *we have not here a lasting city, but we seek one that is to come* (Heb 13:14). We are citizens of heaven, and therefore, led by your grace, "I withdraw to my secret cell and sing you songs of love," my King and my God, "groaning with grief that I cannot express as I journey on my pilgrimage" where your saving acts have become the subjects of my song. "Yet I shall remember the heavenly Jerusalem, and my heart shall be lifted up toward that holy place, Jerusalem my country, Jerusalem my mother. And I shall remember you her Ruler, you who give her light, you her Father, her Guardian," her protector, patron, guide, and shepherd, "you who are her pure, her deep Delight, you who are her constant Joy, you who are at once all that is good beyond the power of words to describe, because you alone are . . . the sovereign Good, the true Good. I shall not turn aside until I come to that abode of peace," Jerusalem "my beloved mother, where my *spiritual harvest* (Rom 8:23) is laid. . . . My God, my Mercy, I shall not turn aside until you gather all that I am . . . rescuing me from this world where I am dismembered and deformed and giving me new form and new strength for eternity."[81]

19

The House of God Is a Created Wisdom, Different from Uncreated Wisdom[82]

our house, Lord, is not an earthly house nor a material edifice in heaven, but is spiritual and shares in your eternity, for it remains firmly established forever.[83] You founded it for the ages, and by your decree it shall not pass away.[84] It is not coeternal with you, because it is not without a beginning but has been created.

Before all other things wisdom was created:[85] not you, O Wisdom who are fully coeternal with the Father and equal to him and in whom all things were created, and the Beginning in which heaven and earth were made,[86] but rather the wisdom that was created, the wisdom that is spiritual in nature and is a light only through contemplation of the Light. Even though created, it is rightly called wisdom; but just as there is a great distance between light that sheds light and light that is a reflection of light, so there is an immense distance between you, the supreme Wisdom that creates, and this other wisdom that is created, or between the Justice that justifies, which you are, O God, and the justice resulting from justification. For according to the apostle, even we are the justice of God the Father in you, his Son and our Lord.[87]

Before all else, then, there was created a wisdom[88] that is the spirit of reason and intelligence of your holy city, our mother, which is on high and is free[89] and exists forever in the heavens (what heavens are these but the heavens of heaven that praise you? For *the heaven of heavens is the Lord's* [Ps 114:16]). There was no time prior to it, for it preceded the creation of time, being the first of all creatures.

Before it there is only you, the eternal God, the Creator of all things, who gave this wisdom its beginning, not indeed in time, since there was no time as yet, but its beginning in its own proper condition. Thus, since it came from you, O God, it is necessarily other than you.

Time did not exist either before it or even in it (for it is able always to see your face and never turns away from it, and therefore undergoes no change). And yet there is in it a certain changeableness so that it would darken and grow cold if it did not cling to you with great love, for it is from you that it derives its midday brightness and warmth. Finally, although it is not coeternal with you, it clings to you, the true and truly eternal God, with a love so pure that not for an instant does it suffer the changes and vicissitudes of time or turn away from you, but rests in perfect contemplation of you alone.

For you, O God, show yourself to this wisdom that loves you as you command, and this is enough for it. Therefore it does not deviate from you or from itself, but remains always in the same state, looking upon you without ceasing and loving you without wearying, O true Light and pure Love.

O happy and sublime creature, greatest of all creatures! "How happy must this creature be . . . constantly intent upon your beatitude!" Happy beyond all telling to be "forever possessed by you, forever bathed in your light! I can think of no description better suited to the Heaven of Heavens, which *belongs to the Lord* (Ps 114:16), than to call it your dwelling which for ever contemplates the blessedness of God, never forsaking it for lesser things, a pure mind at one and undivided in the sure and settled peace of the holy spirits, the heavenly dwellers in your heavenly city far above our earthly heaven.

"In this there is a lesson for the soul, which travels far upon its earthly pilgrimage. If *it thirsts for you*; if *morning and evening its diet is of tears*; if *daily it must listen to the taunt, Where is your God now?* (Ps 42:3-4); if it now *makes one request of you, and one alone, to dwell in your house its whole life long* (Ps 27:4) — and what is its life but you? What are your days but your eternity? What else but eternity are your years, which *can never fail,* because *you are unchanging* (Ps 102:28)? — if this is what it asks, let it learn, as far as it is able, how far above all time you are in your eternity, by reflecting that the heaven of heavens, which is your dwelling and travels upon no worldly pilgrimage, although it is not coeternal with you, nevertheless is free from all vicissitudes of time because it clings to you unfailingly and without cease."[90] By thus drinking from you with persevering purity, this wisdom never shows any sign of change. Because it clings with all its being to your presence, and because it has no future to expect nor past to remember, it knows no change or duration in time.

20

Longing for the House of God, Which Also Prays for Us

 house of light and beauty! *How well I love the house where the Lord dwells, the shrine of his glory!* (Ps 26:8). It is he who made you and it is he who possesses you. In my pilgrimage let me sigh for you,[91] day and night let my heart sigh for you, my spirit strive toward you, and my soul desire to reach a share in your blessedness. I say to him who made you that he should take possession of me within you, for he made me as well. Do you in turn say to him and ask him that he would make me worthy to share in your glory! For I do not expect to share your company and your wonderful beauty because of any merits of mine but because of his blood that has redeemed me; I do not despair of winning you because I am so greatly helped by your merits and aided in my wickedness by your holy and devout and pure prayers which cannot be ineffective with God.

I confess that *I have gone astray like a sheep that is lost* (Ps 119:176) and that *my sojourning is prolonged* (Ps 120:5);[92] I have been cast away, far from the Lord, in this blind exile. Here, expelled from the joys of paradise, I daily sing within me a mournful song of my wretched captivity and I greatly lament as I remember you, Jerusalem my Mother; I stand in your porches, O Zion, holy and beautiful, for I am not yet able, here in the forecourt, to gaze into your inner precincts. Yet I hope that on the shoulders of my

Shepherd, your Builder, I shall be carried within you, there to dance with the ineffable joy of those who join you in the presence of our God and Savior: of him who broke down enmities in his flesh and with his blood brought peace to everything in heaven and on earth. *For he is our peace, who has made both one* (Eph 2:14).[93] When he thus united in himself the two who came face to face, he promised that he would give to both of us, in like manner and equal measure, the lasting happiness of your blessed state, for he said: *They shall be like the angels of God in heaven* (Mt 22:30).

O Jerusalem, everlasting house of God, be our joy and consolation, second only to the love of Christ! May the sweet memory of your blessed name lighten our sadness and weariness!

21

The Miseries of This Life

ord, I am profoundly weary of this life and this burdensome pilgrimage.[94] Yes, this life is a wretched one, transitory, uncertain, laborious, unclean; it is mistress of the wicked, queen of the proud, full of troubles and errors. It should be called not a life but a death, in which at every moment we die many kinds of death due to the failures to which our mutability is liable. Can we truly give the name "life" to what we experience in this world? "Our humors smother it and our pains diminish it; the heat dries it up and the air sickens it; food renders it gross and fasting weakens it; pleasures dissolve it and sorrows eat away at it; worry constricts it, security makes it soft, riches puff it up, poverty casts it down; youth exalts it, old age bows it down, infirmity undermines it, and grief burdens it. And all these evils are followed by raging death that at the same time puts an end to all the joys of this wretched life, so that once they have passed away, it is as if they had never been."[95]

And yet, alas! how many people are snared by the seductions of this living death, this deadly life, despite these and all the other bitter experiences scattered through it, and how many it deceives with its treacherous promises! So intrinsically false and bitter is it that it cannot hide its true nature even from its blind lovers, and yet it gives a countless multitude to drink from the golden cup in its hand and intoxicates them utterly!

Happy they, the few, who flee its company and scorn its superficial joys, and who renounce its fellowship lest they be forced to perish someday along with this deceiver.[96]

22

The Happiness of Eternal Life and the Desire for It

 life that God has prepared for those who love him: life fully alive, life that is happy, secure, tranquil, beautiful, clean, chaste, and holy; life that knows no death or sadness; life that knows no decline or corruption, no sorrow or anxiety, no disturbance, no alteration or change; life of utmost refinement and excellence! In this life there is no enemy, no assailant, and no enticement to sin; there is perfect love and no fear, everlasting and universal harmony of spirits. Here God is seen face to face, and with the food of this life the mind is completely satisfied! It is my pleasure to strain toward your light, and the more capable I become of reflecting on them, the more avidly my heart delights in your blessings. I languish with love of you, am on fire with ardent desire of you, and am filled with delight at the sweet thought of you.

I love, therefore, to raise the eyes of my heart to you, elevate my mind to you, and shape the affections of my soul to harmonize with you. I love to speak and hear and write and converse about you, daily to read of your glorious blessedness, and frequently to mull over in my heart what I have read of you. In this way I am able to turn from the passions and dangers and labors of this mortal and transitory life to the sweet coolness of your life-giving breezes and, when I so turn, to rest my weary head, even if only for a moment, on your bosom. It is for this purpose that I enter the pleasing fields of the sacred scriptures, there to find and pluck the fresh growth of its sentences, to eat by reading and digest by frequent meditation, and finally to gather them all into the deep storehouse of my memory. For by thus tasting your sweetness, I may feel less the bitterness of my wretched life here below.[97]

O life of perfect happiness!

O truly blessed kingdom "which knows no death and has no end and in which through all eternity there is no succession in time! There, everlasting day without night has no experience of time; there the victorious soldier joins in the hymns of the angelic choirs"[98] and sings unceasingly to God the song of the canticles of Zion: "An everlasting crown encircles its noble head."[99] May I be granted forgiveness of my sins and be soon delivered from the burden of this flesh! If only I might enter into your joys and have true rest! If only I might make my way within the splendid, spacious walls of your city and there receive the crown of life from the Lord's hand, "so that I might take my place among those holy choirs, and be present with those blessed spirits to the glory of the Creator, and see before me the face of Christ, and gaze forever on that supreme, indescribable, and unbounded light; then, untouched by any fear of death, I might forever rejoice in the gift of lasting incorruptibility!"[100]

23

The Happiness of the Saints Who Have Passed from This World

appy the soul that has been delivered from its earthly prison and has reached heaven! It is safe there and at peace, and fears neither enemy nor death, for it has its Lord ever present to it and gazes unceasingly on the beauty of him whom it served and loved and whom it has at last reached amid joy and glory. No coming day will lessen this glorious blessedness, no evildoer can take it away. *The daughters saw her and declared her most blessed; the queens and concubines praised her* (Sg 6:8), saying: *Who is this that comes up from the desert, flowing with delights, leaning upon her beloved?* (Sg 8:5). *Who is she that comes forth like the morning rising, fair as the moon, bright as the sun, and terrible as an army set in array?* (Sg 6:9).

How joyously she goes forth, how quickly she runs, when to her astonishment she hears her beloved say to her: *Arise, my friend, my beautiful one, and come. For winter is now past, the rain is over and gone; the flowers have appeared in our land, the time of pruning has come; the voice of the turtle-dove is heard in our land, the fig tree has put forth its green figs, the flowering vines yield their fragrance. Arise, hasten, my friend, my beautiful one, my dove in the clefts of the rock, in the hollows of the wall: show me your face, let your voice sound in my ears. For your voice is sweet and your face lovely* (Sg 2:10-14).

Come, my chosen one, my beautiful one, my dove, my spotless one, my bride!

Come, and I will set my throne within you, for I have desired your beauty!

Come and in my sight rejoice with my angels, whose companionship I have promised you!

Come, after many dangers and toils, and enter into the joy of your Lord, which no one shall take from you.

24

Invocation of the Saints

appy are you, all you saints of God, who have already crossed the sea of this mortal life and deserved to reach the harbor of perpetual rest, safety, and peace.[101] Free of fear and wrapped in calm, you are always festive and joyous.

I beg you in the name of charity, our mother: now that you yourselves have attained security, be concerned for us; now that you are certain of your own unfading glory, be concerned for us in our many afflictions. I beseech you in the name of him who chose you and made you what you now are; whose beauty now satisfies all your desires, whose immortality has made you immortal, and whose blessed vision makes you ever rejoice: be ever mindful of us; help us, your wretched fellows, who are wind-tossed on the sea of this life.

You beautiful gates that are raised so high, help us, the lowly paving stones that lie so far beneath you! Extend your hand and raise us to our feet, so that we may recover from our weakness and become strong in the battle. Intercede for us, pray constantly and without wearying for us poor heedless sinners, that by your prayers we may join your holy company, since otherwise we cannot be saved. For we are very weak: we are puny and powerless individuals, beasts enslaved to stomach and flesh, in whom there is hardly any trace of integrity. And yet because of our faith in Christ we are carried by the wood of the cross as we sail across this deep wide sea in which there are countless reptiles, animals great and small, and the fierce dragon who is always ready to devour. Here too there are places of danger, Charybdis and Scylla[102] and countless others where the heedless and those of wavering faith suffer shipwreck.

Pray for us, then, all you just, pray for us, all you army of saints and throng of the blessed, so that, aided by your prayers, "we may arrive on a safe ship and with unharmed cargo at the harbor of permanent rest, unbroken peace, and unending safety."[103]

25

Ardent Desire for Heaven

other Jerusalem, holy city of God, dear Spouse of Christ, my heart loves you and my spirit greatly desires your beauty. How beautiful, how glorious, how noble you are! You are entirely beautiful and there is no stain in you.

Rejoice and be glad, lovely daughter of the prince, for the king has desired to see your face, and he who is the fairest of the sons of men has loved your beauty.

But, most beautiful one, how does your beloved differ from others? Your *beloved is white and rosy, chosen out of thousands* (Sg 5:9-10). *Like an apple tree in the woods, so is* your *beloved among the sons.* I sit joyfully *in the shadow of him whom I have desired, and his fruit* is *sweet to my palate* (Sg 2:3). *My beloved put his hand through the opening, and my heart trembled at his touch* (Sg 5:4). *In my bed by night I sought my beloved; I sought and found him* (Sg 3:1).

I hold him and will not let him go until he brings me into your house and your chamber, O glorious Mother. For there you will give me your rich breasts[104] more abundantly and completely, and you will satisfy me marvelously, so that I shall no longer hunger or thirst forever.

Happy shall my soul be, happy for all eternity, if I deserve to see your glory, your blessedness, your beauty, your gates and walls, your streets, your many dwellings, your noble citizens, and your mighty King, our Lord, in his glory.

For your walls are made of precious stones, your gates of fine pearls, your streets of purest gold, and in them joyful alleluias ring out unendingly. Your many dwellings have foundations of squared stones and walls of sapphire, and they have roofs of golden tiles; nothing unclean enters them, nothing defiled dwells in them.

You are beautiful and filled with sweet delights, O Mother Jerusalem. There is nothing to be found in you of what we suffer here and what we see during the wretched life of ours. In you there is no darkness, no night, no changing seasons. In you there is no lamp lit, no shining moon, no starlight. Instead, he who is God from God, Light from Light, and Sun of Justice always illumines you; the spotless white Lamb, bright and beautiful, is your light.

Your sun and light and every good you have consists in the unwearying contemplation of this most beautiful King. The King of kings is in your midst, and his children are around you. The choirs of angels are there and the assembly of the citizens of heaven. There, the happy liturgy of those who have ended our sorrowful pilgrimage and reached your joy. There, the wise chorus of the prophets, the brotherhood of the apostles, the victorious army of the countless martyrs, the holy assembly of the confessors, all authentic and perfect monks, all holy women who have overcome the pleasures of the world and the weakness of their sex. There, too, young men and women who have been virtuous beyond their years, and all the sheep and lambs who have escaped the snares of this world's pleasures. All of them rejoice, each of them in their dwelling. The glory of each differs, but all share a common joy. There full and perfect love reigns, for God is *all in all* (1 Cor 15:28). Their vision of him has no end, and as they gaze on him they burn ever more with love. They love and praise, they praise and love. Their entire activity is the praise of God, unending and unwearied.

How happy I will be, happy indeed forever, if after the dissolution of this poor body, I shall deserve to hear the melodious songs of heaven that the citizens of that country on high, the hosts of blessed spirits, sing in praise of the eternal King!

Happy beyond telling will I be if I too deserve to sing these songs and stand before my King, my God, my Leader, and look upon him in his glory, as he deigned to promise that I shall, when he said: *Father, I will that those whom you have given to me may also be with me and see my glory which you gave me before the creation of the world* (Jn 17:24), and elsewhere: *Whoever serve me, let them follow me, and where I am there also shall my servants be* (Jn 12:26), and again: *Those who love me my Father will love, and I will love them and show myself to them* (Jn 14:21).

26

Poem on the Glory of Paradise[105]

For the fount of life unending the parched
spirit thirsts;
the soul in prison seeks to break the bonds of
the flesh;
in exile it glows with desire as it struggles
and seeks the happiness of its own true country.
Meanwhile it groans under burdens and fatigues,
as it contemplates the glory that it lost when it sinned;
present evil renders all the keener
the memory of the good that has been lost.
For who can describe the joy that supreme peace
brings?
There, buildings of living pearls arise,
the lofty roofs gleam with gold,
the dining halls radiate light;
the structure is held together by only precious stones.
The streets are paved with gold as transparent as glass.
No mire there or filth or any contagion.
Frozen winter and scorching summer never rage there.
The red rose marks perpetual spring;
the lilies glow, the crocus reddens, the balsam drips its
perfume,
the meadows are green, the fields yield their growth,
the rivers run with honey.
Ointments emit this fragrance, and spices their fluids.
Fruits that will never fall hang in the blossoming
groves.

The moon, sun, and stars do not run their courses:
the Lamb is the unfailing lamp of this blessed city.
There is no night, no time, but only unbroken day.
There the saints shine like brilliant suns;
crowned after victory they share each other's joy
and, safe now, count the battles they have won over their prostrate foe.
Cleansed now of every stain, they experience no struggles of the flesh.
The flesh that has become spiritual and the mind are at one.
They enjoy abundant peace and serve no more as stumbling-blocks.
Stripped of mutability they turn back to their origin
and contemplate the ever-present face of truth,
and from it derive the life-giving sweetness of the fount of life.
Therefore their existence is ever unchanged;
filled with light and life and pleasure,
they suffer no mishaps.
Always healthy, they know no illness;
always young, no old age. So their being never ends, for transitoriness itself has passed away.
They are ever green and active and in their flower; corruption has vanished,
the power of immortality has absorbed the power of death.
They know him who knows all, and can be ignorant of nothing.
They penetrate the secret places of each other's hearts;
they are one in what they will and what they reject,
for their thoughts are in harmony.
Though the merits of each differ according to their work on earth,
charity makes its own what it loves in the other.
The good of each becomes the good of all.

Where the carcass is, the eagles rightly gather.
So saintly souls are refreshed with the angels.
The citizens of these two countries live on the same bread;
they are hungry yet always filled,
and they desire what they possess.
Abundance never brings aversion nor does hunger torment them;
they are always hungry when they eat,
and eating leaves them hungry still.
The tuneful voice produces harmonies ever new,
and instruments caress the ear with exultant song.
The saints sing praises to the King who made them victors.
Happy the soul that sees the King of heaven face to face
and from its place on high looks down upon the revolving elements of the world:
the sun, the moon, and the rounded stars with the planets.
O Christ, reward of those who fight,
lead me into this city
when I have put off my soldier's belt;
give me a share in the gratuity bestowed on the blessed.
Strengthen me who toil now in the unending battle,
so that when I have served my time
you may owe me rest after the struggle
and I may possess you, my reward, forever more.
Amen.[106]

27

Praising God with the Blessed[107]

less the Lord, my soul, and let all that is within me bless his holy name. Bless the Lord, my soul, and forget not all his benefits to you (Ps 103:1-2).

Bless the Lord, all his works; bless the Lord, my soul, in every place where he rules. Let us praise the Lord whom the Angels praise and the Dominations adore, and before whom the Powers tremble; whom the Cherubim and Seraphim ceaselessly proclaim as "Holy, Holy Holy!"

Let us join our voices to the voices of the holy angels and praise our one Lord as best we can. They praise the Lord in utter purity and unceasingly, because they contemplate our God not as in a mirror and obscurely but face to face.

But who can put into words or conceive of "this countless throng of blessed spirits and heavenly powers that stand in the presence of almighty God, their endless jubilation in the vision of God, their unfailing joy, the fire of love that does not torment but delights them, their yearning for the vision even as it satisfies them and their satisfaction even as they yearn; in them desire does not cause pain nor does satisfaction bring distaste. Who can imagine how they attained blessedness by possessing him who is supreme blessedness, or how they have become light by union with the true Light, or how they are changed into changelessness by gazing constantly on the changeless Trinity?"[108]

But how shall we ever be able to understand the lofty dignity of the angels, when we are unable to fathom the nature of our own soul?

What is this soul that is able to give life to the flesh, yet cannot limit itself to holy thoughts as it wishes to do?

What is this soul that is so strong and so weak, so little and so great, that penetrates secrets and contemplates the heavens, while also displaying outstanding genius and skill in the many arts that profit human beings?

What, then, is this soul that knows so much of other things but is utterly ignorant of its own nature? For although not a few dubious opinions are proposed about its origin, we may think nonetheless that it is an intellectual spirit brought into being by the Creator's power; that it lives for ever in its own manner, but also gives life to the mortal body which it keeps in being but which is subject to change and destined for oblivion; that it is often cast down by fear and exalted by joy. What a wonderful and utterly astonishing thing the soul is!

Of God, the Creator of all, who is incomprehensible and ineffable, we read, speak, and write things lofty and wonderful without the slightest hesitation; yet we are not so sure of anything we say about angels and souls.[109]

But, my spirit, turn away from all that; rise above all created things, run and ascend, fly and pass beyond, and direct the eyes of faith as far as you can to him who created all things. I shall climb a ladder within my heart and by way of my soul I shall ascend to my God, who dwells above me. All visible sights, all spiritual imaginings I shall resolutely thrust far away from my spirit's gaze. Then let the pure and simple intellect alone soar quickly aloft and reach the Creator of angels and souls and all else that is.

Happy the spirit that abandons the depths and seeks the heights; that sets up its dwelling on high and from the peaks contemplates with eagle eyes the Sun of justice. For nothing is as pleasing, nothing as delightful, as to contemplate God with the mind's eye alone and with a thirsting heart, and in a wonderful way to see, invisibly, the invisible One. Thus one tastes a different joy and sees a different light than the joy and light of this present world. For our light here is enclosed in space, limited in time, and interrupted by night, and we share it with worms and cattle; by comparison with that supreme light it is less light than night.

Stimulus to the Praise of God[110]

lthough that supreme, changeless essence — the true and unfailing Light that shines upon the angels — cannot be seen by anyone in this life, being reserved as a reward for the saints in glory, yet to believe in it and understand and recognize it and long for it with great desire is already to possess it in a way.

Let our voices therefore be heard above the angels, and let us human beings contemplate God with attentive spirit and sing his praises in whatever words we can. For it is right that creatures should praise the Creator, since he made us in order that we might praise him, though he has no need of our praises. His greatness is beyond our comprehension; he needs nothing and is sufficient to himself. *Great is our Lord and great his power, and his wisdom is beyond measure* (Ps 146:5); *the Lord is great and exceedingly to be praised* (Ps 95:4).

Let every heart love him, then, every tongue praise him, every hand write of him, and every faithful soul devote itself wholly to these sacred pursuits.

Let the *man of desires* (Dn 9:23) and contemplator of things heavenly feed constantly at the delightful banquet of heavenly study, so that, strengthened by this heavenly nourishment, he may cry out with a loud voice, with all his heart, in jubilation, and with intense spiritual desire:

Praise of the Countless Wonders of God

upreme One, all-powerful, merciful yet just, hidden yet present, beautiful and strong, you are immovable and incomprehensible.[111] You are invisible but see everything, "unchanging but you effect all change; immortal, not restricted by place, unbounded, uncircumscribed, and unlimited; beyond all estimation, ineffable, impenetrable, unmoved by anything yet touching everything.

You are unsearchable, inexpressible, fearful and terrible, to be honored and inspiring terror; never old, never new, making all things new, bringing the proud to destruction though they know it not; always active, always at rest; gathering though you have no need, sustaining everything though feeling no burden, filling all things without being confined by any, creating and preserving everything, nourishing it and bringing it to completion, seeking, though you lack for nothing.

You love without passion, you are zealous yet at peace, you regret without suffering, you are angry yet remain calm; you change your works but not your plan.

You receive what you find but have never lost; you are never in need, yet rejoice in what you gain; you are never greedy, yet you demand interest; you go further and become a debtor, yet what does anyone have that is not yours? You pay your debts though you owe nothing to anyone, you pay your debts but you lose nothing.[112]

You alone give life to all things, you create them, you are everywhere and wholly everywhere; you can be known but not seen; though you are everywhere, you are far removed from the thoughts of the wicked; you are there even though you are far off, for where you are not present by your grace, you are present in punishment.

You act upon all things, but not upon all things equally. Some you act upon to make them be but not to have life and consciousness; others you act upon to make them be and live but not to have consciousness and understanding; still others you act upon to make them be and live and have consciousness, but not to have understanding; and others, finally, you act upon to make them be and live and have consciousness and understanding.

Although you never differ from yourself, you deal differently with different things.[113] You are everywhere present, are difficult to find. We follow you, who do not move away, but we cannot lay hold of you. You hold and fill and surround and transcend and sustain all things.

You do not support in part and transcend in part, nor do you fill in part and surround in part; rather you fill by surrounding and surround by filling, you transcend as you sustain and sustain as you transcend. You teach the hearts of the faithful without audible words.

You *reach from end to end mightily and order all things sweetly* (Wis 8:1). You are not extended by space nor changed by time. You do not come and go but *dwell in inaccessible light and no one has ever seen or can see you* (1 Tm 6:16).

You remain at rest in yourself, yet encircle the universe at every point. You cannot be broken or divided, for you are truly one; nor can you be separated into parts for with your whole self you hold and fill and illumine and possess everything.

The human mind cannot grasp the immensity and depth of this mystery; no eloquence can express it nor can libraries of volumes with their spacious discourse. Books

83

might fill the entire world, but your indescribable knowledge would still elude description.

For you are truly ineffable; no word can describe or capture you, who are the fountain of divine light and the sun of eternal brightness. For you are great without any element of quantity, and therefore immeasurable. You are good, but not composed of any qualities, and therefore truly and supremely good.

No one is good save you alone, whose will and action are one, and whose willing is power. By your simple will you made all the things which you created out of nothing. You possess all your creatures though you need none of them; you govern without effort and rule without labor, and nothing in the heights or in the depths disturbs your orderly dominion.

You are in all places without being contained by place; you contain all things without having to surround them; you are present in every place without residing there or moving to it. You are not the author of evil, which you cannot do though you can do everything.

Never have you regretted doing anything, nor are you disturbed by any surge of feeling. Your rule extends not to a part of the world but to the entire universe. You neither approve nor command crime and sin. You never lie, for you are eternal Truth. Your goodness alone created us, your justice punishes us, your mercy sets us free. Nothing heavenly or fiery or earthly, nothing that touches our bodily senses, is to be worshiped in your place.

You truly are what you are and do not change. To you most of all and in a unique way applies the Greek term *ôn*, the Latin *est*, for *you are always the same, and your years shall not fail* (Ps 102:28).

"This and much more has been taught me by Holy Mother Church, whose member I have become by your grace."[114] She has taught me that you, the only living and true God, are neither corporeal nor passible nor sensible;

that nothing in your substance or nature is in any way vulnerable or changeable; it is in no way composite or put together. Therefore it is certain that bodily eyes cannot see you, and no mortal has ever been able to see your essence.

It is clear, then, that as the angels see you, so too we shall see you after this present life. But not even they can see you perfectly as you are; to no one but yourself alone is the omnipotent Trinity known.

30

Prayer to the Blessed Trinity

ou, the one Godhead, are multiple in your plurality of persons; you cannot be counted, yet you are three, and therefore you are measurable in your immeasurableness and can be appraised in your very inappraisableness. We do not claim, then, an origin for your supreme goodness, from which, through which, and in which all things are; we say rather that all things are good by participation in this goodness. For your divine substance always has been and now is without matter, although it does not lack a form, namely an unformed form, the form of all forms, the most beautiful of all forms;[115] even as you impress this form like a seal on all existent things, you make them utterly different from yourself without any change that would lessen or augment your being.

All the creatures that exist in nature are your creatures, O God, one Trinity and triune Oneness!

"Your omnipotence possesses, governs, and fills everything it has created. We do not mean, however, that because you fill all things, they contain you, but rather that they are contained by you. Nor do you fill things with part of yourself; we must not think that each creature receives you in proportion to its size, as though the larger had more of you and the smaller less, for your whole self is in everything, or rather all things are in you. Your omnipotence embraces all things, nor has any creature ever found a way of escaping from your power. For those that do not have your favor will not escape your anger, as it is written: *Neither from the East nor from the West nor from the desert hills, for God is the judge* (Ps 75:7-8), and elsewhere: *Whither shall I go from your spirit? or whither shall I flee from your face?* (Ps 139:7).

"The immensity of your greatness is such that you are in all things but not contained by them and are above all things but not excluded from them."[116] "You are within all things that you may contain them; you are outside of all things so that you may embrace them in your limitless immensity. Because you are external to them, you show that you are their Creator; because you are interior to them, you show that you govern them all. And lest created things be without you, you are both within them all and outside them all, not by any extension in place but by the presence of your power. You are everywhere present, and all are present to you. Some of these creatures understand this, others do not."[117]

The oneness of your indivisible nature does not permit the persons to be separated, for since the Trinity exists in unity and the Unity in trinity, there can be in you no separation of persons. It is said at times that each person has its unique character; but, O Triune God, you have made known the fact that the persons are inseparable by giving each a name which indicates that it exists only in relation to another; thus the Father is related to the Son, the Son to the Father, and the Holy Spirit to the Father and the Son. On the other hand, the names signifying your substance or power or essence belong equally to all the persons: God, great, omnipotent, eternal, and all the other predicates applied to your nature as God. There is therefore no name signifying your nature that can belong to you, God the Father, in such a way as not to belong also to your Son or the Holy Spirit.

We say that you, the Father, are by nature God, but the Son too is by nature God and the Holy Spirit is by nature

God. Yet there are not three Gods, but Father, Son, and Holy Spirit possessing the one divine nature.

For this reason, O holy Trinity of God, we must understand that your persons are inseparable, even though they have different names, for you do not have different names for your nature. This shows that the persons cannot be divided in the holy Trinity, which is one true God, for the name of each person is always related to another person. If I say "the Father," I make clear that there is a Son; if I name the Son, I proclaim the Father; if I invoke the Holy Spirit, he must be understood to be someone's Spirit, namely, the Father's and the Son's.

This is the true faith which comes to us through sound teaching; this is, beyond doubt, the catholic and orthodox faith which your grace, O God, has taught me in the bosom of Mother Church.[118]

31

Invocation of the Holy Trinity

 or this reason, Lord, I call upon you with the faith which you in your goodness have given me for my salvation. The faithful soul lives by faith and clings in hope to what it will see in its reality.

My God, I call upon you with a pure conscience and with the sweet love which is inspired by my faith, this faith which you have brought to an understanding of the truth by dispelling the darkness and which you have made pleasant and indeed honey-sweet for me by removing the bitterness of worldliness and filling it in faith with the sweetness of your love.

O blessed Trinity, I call upon you in a loud voice and with the heartfelt love inspired by my faith, the faith which you have nourished in me from my cradle and which you have enlightened with the light of your grace, the faith which you have intensified and made strong in me through the teaching of Mother Church.[119]

I call upon you, O one, beatific, blessed, and glorious Trinity, who are "Father and Son and Holy Spirit; God, Lord, and Paraclete; charity, grace, and communication; begetter, begotten, and giver of rebirth; true light, true light from light, and true enlightenment; fountain, river, and inflooding; from one all things, through one all things, in one all things; from whom all things, through whom all things, in whom all things; living life, life from living life, giver of life to all who live; one from himself, one from that one, one from both; *ôn*[120] from himself, *ôn* from the other, *ôn* from both; truthful Father, Son who is Truth, Holy Spirit who is Truth. Father, Logos,[121] and Paraclete are thus one essence, one power, one goodness."[122]

32

Invocation and Praise of God

God, supreme and true beatitude,
by whom, through whom, and in whom all
creatures have their blessedness!
O God, true and supreme life, from whom,
through whom, and in whom
all creatures that truly live and are blessed have their life!
O God, good and beautiful,
from whom, through whom, and in whom
all good and beautiful creatures have their goodness
and beauty!
O God, who awaken us by faith,
raise us up by hope,
and unite us by love!
O God, who command us to seek you
and help us to find you
and open to us when we knock!
O God, to turn away from whom is to fall,
to turn to whom is to rise up,
to remain in whom is to perdure!
O God, whom no one loses save by self-deception,
whom no one seeks save by repenting,
and whom no one finds except by being purified!
O God, to know whom is to live,
to serve whom is to reign,
and to praise whom is the soul's salvation and joy![123]
I praise, bless, and adore you
with lips and heart and all my strength;

I thank you for all the blessings of your mercy and goodness,
and I sing a hymn to your glory: Holy, Holy, Holy.
I call upon you,
O blessed Trinity:
come to me
and make me a temple worthy of your glory!
I ask the Father through the Son,
I ask the Son through the Father,
I ask the Holy Spirit through the Father and the Son,[124]
to take all the vices from me
and to plant in me all the holy virtues.
Infinite God,
by whom all things,
through whom all things,
and in whom all things, visible and invisible,
have been made,
you who surround and fill and protect and sustain your
works,
protect me, who am the work of your hands;
I place my hope in you, and in your mercy alone I trust.
Protect me, I pray, here and everywhere,
now and always,
within me and without,
before me and behind,
above me and below,
and all around me,
so that at no point am I exposed to the snares of the enemy.
You are God almighty,
guardian and protector of all who hope in you;
apart from you no one is safe,
no one free of danger.
You are God, and there is no god beside you,
neither in the heavens above nor on the earth below;
your works are great and wonderful,
beyond comprehension and beyond numbering.

33

Those Who Desire to Praise
Inquire How They Are to Praise

t is right to praise you, it is right to glorify you. All the angels, the heavens and all the powers chant hymns to you and ceaselessly join in singing your praises, as creatures to their Creator, servants to their Lord, and soldiers to their captain. Every creature glorifies you, the holy and undivided Trinity, every spirit praises you. The saints and the humble of heart, the spirits and souls of the just, all the citizens of heaven and all the orders of blessed spirits humbly worship you and sing unceasing praises of your glory and honor. "Let human beings, who are so great a part of your creation, praise you."[125]

I too, a poor sinner, ardently desire to praise you; I want to love you beyond all things else.

My God, my life, my strength, and my praise, make me worthy to praise you. Enlighten my heart and put words in my mouth, so that my heart may contemplate your glory and my tongue sing your praises all day long.

But because *praise is not seemly in the mouth of a sinner* (Sir 15:9) and because *I am a man of unclean lips* (Is 6:5), purify my mouth of all uncleanness, I beg you. Almighty Sanctifier, make me holy inwardly and outwardly, and make me worthy to praise you.

In your kindness accept from my heart's hand and with my mind's love the sacrifice of my lips; let it become acceptable in your sight and rise to you as a pleasing fragrance. Let the devout remembrance of you and your sweet blessedness take possession of my entire soul and carry it up to love of things invisible. Let my soul pass from the visible world to the invisible, from earth to heaven, from time to eternity; let it pass over and see the wonderful vision.

"Eternal Truth, true Love, beloved Eternity — all this, my God, you are, and it is to you that I sigh night and day."[126] I long for you, I reach out to you, I desire to come to you. Those who know you know truth and eternity. You who are Truth rule over everything, and we shall see you as you are (1 Jn 3:2),[127] when this blind mortal life shall have passed away, during which we hear men ask: *"Where is your God?"* (Ps 42:3). And I too say: "My God, where are you?" I rest a little in you, when I pour out my soul in jubilation and confess you in songs of festive celebration. But my soul is saddened again, for it falls back and becomes an abyss or rather is aware that it is still an abyss.

But then my faith, which you light as a fire in the night to guide my feet, says to me: *Why are you sad, my soul, and why do you trouble me?* (Ps 43:5). Hope in the Lord, for his word is a lamp for my feet. Hope and persevere until night, the mother of the wicked, has passed; until the Lord's wrath has passed, that wrath of which we were once the children, for at one time we were darkness; until this darkness completely disappears, the remnants of which we still carry in our bodies that are dead because of sin. Hope in the Lord until day is near and the shadows withdraw. On that morning I shall stand before you and contemplate you and forever place my trust in you.

In the morning I will stand before you and will see (Ps 5:4) the salvation of my face, my God, who *will give life to* our *mortal bodies because of the Spirit who dwells in* us (Rom 8:11). And so we are already light, we are already saved in hope; we are *the children of light and children of the day, not of the night nor of darkness* (1 Thes 5:5). For we *were at one time darkness but now are light* in you, our God (Eph 5:8). But we are still light only through faith, not through vision. Hope that sees is not hope.

Lord, let the immortal angelic peoples praise you, and the supercelestial Powers glorify your name, for they have no need of reading our scriptures in order to know you as the holy and indivisible Trinity. For they always see your face and in it they read, without any sequence of words, what your eternal will is. They read, they choose, they love. They are always reading, and what they read never passes from their minds. They choose and they love as they read your changeless plan. Their manuscript has no end, nor shall their book be finished, for you yourself are their book and will be for eternity.

How blessed indeed are the Powers of heaven, who are able to praise in a holy and pure manner with ecstatic sweetness and ineffable jubilation! What they praise is also the source of their joy, for they see always that which enables them both to rejoice and to praise. But we are not able to praise you as you deserve while we are weighed down by the burden of the flesh and live far from your face on this earthly pilgrimage, divided and torn by the constant changes of this world. We walk by faith and not yet by vision, while those angelic spirits walk by vision and not by faith. This is why our praise is so different from theirs. But despite our different ways of praising you, you remain the one God and Creator of all, to whom the sacrifice of praise is offered in heaven and on earth. By your mercy we shall attain to their company, and with them we shall see you always and praise you forever.

Lord, grant that while I live in this weak body, my heart and tongue may praise you, and all my bones say: *Lord, who is like you?* (Ex 15:11).

You are almighty God, whom we worship and adore as three in persons and one in your divine substance: Father unbegotten, Son begotten of the Father, Holy Spirit proceeding from both and remaining in both. When we did not exist, you used your power and made us; and when we were lost by our sins, you marvelously restored us because you are faithful and good.

I beg you, do not allow us to be ungrateful for such great blessings and unworthy of your many mercies. I pray, beg, and beseech you: increase our faith, our hope, our love. By your grace make us always firm in faith and active in deeds, so that because of a right faith and deeds worthy of faith we may through your mercy reach eternal life. There we shall see your glory as it is and adore your majesty, and we shall say, with those whom you have rendered worthy of seeing your limitless beauty:

"Glory to the Father who made us! Glory to the Son who redeemed us! Glory to the Holy Spirit who has sanctified us!"[128] Glory to the perfect and undivided Trinity, whose activities are inseparable and whose reign remains forever. It is right to praise you and glorify you, for all glory is due you.

To you, our God, be blessing and splendor, to you be thanksgiving, to you be honor, power, and strength through endless ages. Amen.

34

Humble Confession of a Sinner Who Is Unworthy to Offer Praise[129]

orgive me, Lord, forgive me in your kindness, forgive me and have mercy; spare me in my ignorance and my many imperfections.

Do not reject me for my boldness in daring to call myself your servant and desiring even to be a good one and not simply an *unprofitable servant* (Lk 17:10) and a wicked one, and therefore evil, very evil indeed.

Do not reject me if I praise, bless, and adore you, our almighty, awesome, and greatly to be feared God, without contrition of heart and flowing tears and without due reverence and fear.

If the very angels tremble even as they adore and praise you and are filled with wondrous exultation, why is it that when I, a sinner, am in your presence singing praise and offering sacrifice, I am not terrified in my heart and my face does not grow pale, my lips do not tremble, and my whole body is not agitated, nor do I constantly grieve before you amid tears? I want to approach you in this way, but I am not able. And, seeing with the eyes of faith that you are so greatly to be feared, I am filled with amazement that I cannot do as I desire.

But who can approach you in this way without the help of your grace? Our entire salvation is a great mercy on your part. What a wretch I am!

How has my soul become so unfeeling that it is not terror-struck when it stands before God and sings its praises to him? What a wretch I am!

How has my heart become so hardened that my eyes do not produce unceasing floods of tears as the servant converses with his Lord, the human being with his God, the creature with his Creator, one *formed of the slime of the earth* (Gn 2:7) with him who made all things out of nothing?

See, Lord, I set myself before you and do not try to hide from your fatherly ear what I know myself to be in the depths of my being.

You are *rich in mercy* (Eph 2:4) and generous in your rewards: grant me the blessings that will enable me to serve you, for it is only through your gift that we can serve and please you. Pierce my flesh with fear of you; let my heart find joy in fearing your name. Would that my sinful soul might fear you as that holy man did who said: *I have always feared God as waves swelling over me* (Jb 31:23).

God, giver of all gifts, grant me a fountain of tears, purity of heart, and jubilation of spirit as I praise you, so that I may love you perfectly and praise you as you deserve and so with the palate of my heart experience and taste and savor your sweetness, Lord, as it is written: *Taste and see that the Lord is sweet; blessed are they who hope in him* (Ps 34:9). *Blessed the people who know jubilation* (Ps 88:16). *Blessed they whose help is from you; in their hearts they have made ready to ascend by steps, here in the valley of tears, in the place in which you have set them* (Ps 84:6-7). *Blessed are the clean of heart, for they shall see God* (Mt 5:8). *Blessed are they who dwell in your house, Lord; they shall praise you forever and ever* (Ps 84:5).

35

Prayer Inspired by
Fervent Love of Jesus[130]

esus, our Redeemer, object of my love and desire, God from God, be with me, your servant! I call to you, I cry out to you in a loud voice, and with all my heart I call you into my soul; enter into it, mold it to your likeness so that you may possess it as a soul without spot or wrinkle. For the dwelling of the most pure Lord must itself be pure. Therefore sanctify me as the vessel which you made for yourself; rid it of sin, fill it with grace, and keep it full. Thus I will become a worthy temple for you to dwell in, here and for all eternity.

You are sweet and kind and loving, dear and precious and desirable, lovable and beautiful; sweeter than honey, whiter than milk or snow, more pleasing to my soul than nectar, more priceless than precious stones and gold, and dearer to me than all the riches and honors of this world.

What am I saying, my God, my only hope, my mercy beyond compare?

What am I saying, O sweetness that never disappoints, O sweetness that makes me happy and secure?

What am I saying when I say these things? I am saying what I can but not what I ought.

If only I could sing hymns like the hymns of the angelic choirs! How joyously I would then pour myself out in praise of you! How devoutly and unceasingly, here in the midst of the Church, I would sing those heavenly melodies to the praise and glory of your name! But shall I fall silent because I cannot sing such songs? Woe to those who remain silent about you, you who open the mouths of the dumb and make eloquent the tongues of children! Woe to those who remain silent about you, for even those who speak are dumb when they sing your praises!

Who can worthily praise you, O ineffable Power and Wisdom of the Father? And because I find no words that can adequately express you, O omnipotent and omniscient Word, let me say for the moment what I can, until you bid me come to you, where I will indeed be able to say what befits you and is my duty. Therefore I humbly ask you to look not so much to what I say now as to what I desire to say.

For I greatly desire to speak of you as I ought and as is right. It is right to praise and sing hymns to you; to you all honor is due. You are God, who knows all that is hidden, and you know not only that you are dearer to me than earth and all it contains but also that you are more pleasing and lovable to me than heaven itself and all that is in it. For I love you more than heaven and earth and all that is in them; indeed, were it not for love of your name, things transitory would not be lovable at all.

I love you, my God, with a great love, and I desire to love you more and more. Grant that I may always love you as much as I desire and ought, so that you alone may be the object of my attention and meditation.

Let me meditate on you day after day without ceasing; let me be aware of you in my nightly sleep; let my spirit speak to you, my mind converse with you, and my heart be enlightened by the light of the holy vision of you. Thus, under your lead and guidance I will advance from virtue to virtue and will at last see you, *the God of gods, in Zion* (Ps 84:8). I see you now indeed *as in a mirror, dimly, but then face to face*, when *I shall know even as I am known* (1 Cor 13:12). *Blessed are the clean of heart, for they shall see God*

(Mt 5:8). *Blessed are they who dwell in your house, Lord; they shall praise you forever and ever* (Ps 84:5).

I beseech you, therefore, Lord, in the name of all the mercies by which you have delivered us from everlasting death, that you would soften my heart of hard stone and iron with your powerful holy anointing. In the fire of compunction make me at every hour a living sacrifice before you.

Grant me a contrite and humble heart in your sight, a heart filled with abundant tears.

Grant that out of desire of you I may die utterly to this world and out of great fear and love of you I may forget all transitory things. Then I shall no longer either lament or rejoice over the things of time, no longer either fear or love anything temporal; I shall not be seduced by pleasure nor cast down by adversity.

And because the fullness of your *love is strong as death* (Sg 8:6), let the fiery and sweet power of your love draw my mind away from all things under heaven, so that I may adhere to you alone and feed solely on the sweet memory of you.

Lord, I pray you, let your sweet fragrance penetrate deep, deep into my heart; let your love that is sweet as honey enter into it. Let the indescribably wonderful fragrance of your very self come over me that it may rouse everlasting desires in me and from my heart make streams of water gush forth for everlasting life. You are beyond measure, Lord, and ought to be loved and praised without measure by those whom you have redeemed with your precious blood, O kindly lover of humanity!

Most merciful Lord and most impartial judge, to whom *the Father has given all judgment* (Jn 5:22), by a most wise decree of your justice you determine it to be right and equitable that the children of this present world of night and darkness should love and seek perishable riches and fleeting honors with great desire and energetic zeal, more so than we your servants love you, our God, who made and redeemed us.[131] For if two human beings can love one another so much that each can only with difficulty endure the absence of the other; if a wife is so ardently attached to her husband that her great love will not let her rest and she endures great sadness at the absence of her beloved: with what love and passion and fervor should not the soul which you have espoused to yourself in justice and fidelity, in mercy and compassion, love you, the true God and incomparably beautiful husband, you who so loved and saved us and have done such many wonderful things for us?

Things here below have indeed their pleasures and their charms, but they do not delight us as you, our God, do. For in you the just find their delight, because love of you is sweet and serene; it pours sweetness and delight and tranquillity into the hearts of which it takes possession. Worldly and fleshly love, however, is full of anxiety and trouble; it does not allow the souls into which it enters to be at peace, but constantly worries them with suspicions and uneasiness and fears of every kind. You therefore are the delight of the just, and rightly so, for in you they find deep peace and an untroubled life. They who enter into you, our good Lord, enter into the joy of their Lord; they shall no longer fear but will be utterly blessed, as they say: *This is my rest forever and ever; here will I dwell, for I have chosen it* (Ps 132:14), and again: *The Lord is my shepherd, I shall not want for anything; he has set me in a place of pasture* (Ps 23:1).

Sweet Christ, good Jesus, always fill my heart with an inextinguishable love of you and the continual thought of you, so that I may be set utterly on fire with a sweet love of you that many waters can never quench in me.

Sweet Lord, grant that I may love you and in my desire for you may shake off the heavy burden of fleshly lusts that attack and weigh down my wretched soul. Thus freed, I shall run after the fragrance of your perfumes until under your guidance I quickly attain to the satisfying vision of your beauty.

Two loves, one good and the other evil, one sweet and the other bitter, cannot dwell together in the same heart. Those who love anything other than you, O God, do not have your love in them. Love of sweetness and sweetness of love; love that does not torment but delights, love that is heartfelt and pure, abiding forever: "Love ever burning, never quenched!"[132]

Sweet Christ, good Jesus, my God who is Love, set me wholly on fire with your fire, with love of you and sweet delight in you, with well-being and joy in you, with pleasurable desire of you, a desire that is holy and good, chaste and pure, tranquil and untroubled.

Then, wholly filled with sweet love of you and wholly engulfed in the flame of charity, I shall love you, my Lord, with all my heart and everything that is in me. I shall have you in my heart and on my lips and always and everywhere before my eyes, so that there will be no room left in me for adulterous loves.

Listen to me, my God! Listen to me, light of my eyes! Listen to what I ask of you, and grant that I may ask for what you can give.

Faithful Lord who are moved by prayer, do not cease to be moved because of my sins, but because of your own goodness receive the prayers of your servant, and grant me what I ask and desire, through the intercession and prayers and petitions of your glorious Mother, my Lady, and of all the saints. Amen.

36

Prayer to Christ with Desire for Love and Tears[133]

ord Christ, Word of the Father, who came into this world to save sinners, I ask you in the name of your great mercy: correct my life, improve my actions, reform my conduct, and take from me what harms me and displeases you; grant me what you know pleases you and profits me. Who but you alone can make clean what has been conceived of unclean seed?

You are almighty God and your faithfulness is unlimited; you justify the wicked and give life to the dead; you change sinners and they are no longer sinners. Take from me, therefore, whatever in me is displeasing to you; for even my eyes see much that is imperfect in me.

Extend your loving hand, I pray, and take from me whatever is offensive in the sight of your goodness. You have before you both my health and my sickness; preserve my health and heal my sickness. *Heal me, O Lord, and I shall be healed; save me and I shall be saved* (Jer 17:14), for it is you who heal the infirm and preserve them in health; it is you who by your mere command restore what has fallen in ruins. For if you deign to sow good seed in your field, then you must first tear out with loving hands the thorns of my vices.

Sweet, kind, living, dear, precious, desirable, lovable, and beautiful Lord, pour into my heart, I beg you, your most sweet love, so that I may not desire or think upon anything earthly or fleshly, but may love you alone and have you alone in my heart and on my lips. With your finger inscribe in my breast the sweet memory of your honeyed name, never to be erased by forgetfulness. Write your will and your saving love on the tablets of my heart, so that I may always and everywhere keep my eyes fixed on you, my infinitely sweet Lord, and on your commandments. Inflame my spirit with the fire that you sent upon the earth and willed should blaze up mightily.[134] Then I shall daily offer to you amid tears the sacrifice of an afflicted spirit and a contrite heart.

Sweet Christ, good Jesus, grant me what I desire and ask with all my heart: that I be filled and grasped and wholly possessed by a holy and chaste love of you. And grant me this clear sign of your love for me: an ever-flowing fountain of tears, so that these tears may bear witness to my love of you. Let them reveal, let them say, how much my soul loves you, with a love so great that its sweetness compels me to weep.

I recall, Lord, that good woman of whom scripture speaks, who came to your sanctuary to ask for a son and whose countenance, after she had wept and prayed, was no longer sad.[135] But when I think of such great virtue and perseverance, I am pained and shamed and abashed, for I see how inferior to her I am in my wretchedness. For if a woman who wanted a son could thus weep and persevere in her sorrow, how much more should the soul constantly lament that seeks and loves God and desires to attain to him? Should not the soul that desires to love Christ and him alone mourn and weep night and day? Astonishing indeed is it if tears have not become this soul's food day and night.

Look mercifully upon me, then, for my heart's sorrows have been multiplied.

Grant me your heavenly consolation and do not reject my sinful soul, since for it, too, you died.

Grant me the interior tears that spring from love of you and that can break the bonds of my sins and fill my soul with heavenly delight.[136] Thus I may merit to obtain some little place in your heavenly kingdom, if not with true and perfect monks, in whose footsteps I am unable to follow, at least with holy women.

I also think of the marvelous devotion of another woman, the one who with faithful love sought you as you lay in the tomb. When the disciples departed from the tomb, she did not leave but sat there for a long time, sad and mournful and weeping copious tears. She would repeatedly rise up amid her tears and with watchful eyes explore all the corners of the tomb, in case she might be able to see you whom she was seeking with such fervent desire. She had already gone repeatedly to look at the tomb, but this was not enough for so great a lover, for it is perseverance that makes a good deed efficacious.[137]

It was because she loved you above all else and because she sought you amid tears and persevered in her search that she was to meet you and see you and speak to you.[138] More than that: she was the first to announce your glorious resurrection even to your disciples, for in your mercy you urged and ordered her: *Go and tell my brothers that they are to go into Galilee; there they shall see me* (Mt 28:10). If, then, this woman, who sought you living among the dead and did not touch you with the hand of faith, shed so many tears and persevered in weeping, how much more should souls weep and continue weeping who believe in their hearts and confess with their tongues that you are their Redeemer, already sitting in heaven and ruling everywhere? How much more should souls lament and weep who love you with all their heart and whose whole desire is to see you?

O sole refuge and only hope of the wretched, to whom no one ever prays without hope of mercy, grant me this favor for your own sake and for the sake of your holy name: that as often as I think of you or speak of you or write of you or read about you or discuss you, as often as I remember you or enter your presence or offer you praise, prayer, and sacrifice, I may on every occasion weep copious sweet tears, so that tears may become my bread day and night.

It was you yourself, King of glory and Teacher of all the virtues, who taught us, by word and example, to mourn and weep, for you said: *Blessed are they that mourn, for they shall be comforted* (Mt 5:5). You yourself wept for your dead friend,[139] and you wept over the city that was to be destroyed.[140]

Good Jesus, I ask you by those blessed tears of yours and by all the wonderful mercies with which you have deigned to come to our aid when we were lost: grant me the gift of tears, which my soul so desires and pleads for, for it is only by your gift that I can have such tears.

Through your Holy Spirit, who softens the hard hearts of sinners and pierces them to the point of tears, grant me the gift of tears, as you gave it to my forefathers in whose steps I should follow. Then will I lament my state all my life as they did, day and night. For the sake of the merits and prayers of these forebears who served you with utmost devotion and were pleasing to you, have mercy on me, your most wretched and unworthy servant, and grant me the gift of tears.

Grant me a supply of tears like the early rains and the late rains, so that tears may become my bread day and night.

My God, may the fire of compunction make of my inmost being a rich holocaust in your sight. Let me be wholly immolated on the altar of my heart, and accept me as a rich holocaust that pleases you with its fragrance.

Grant me a flowing, a crystal-clear fountain in which to wash this sullied sacrifice. The truth is that although I offer myself entirely to you with the help of your grace, I nonetheless offend you daily in many ways because of my excessive weakness.

Grant me, therefore, O blessed God who are so deserving of love, the gift of tears: tears that flow from the great sweetness of love of you and from the remembrance of your mercies. Prepare this table for your servant and in the sight of your servant, and place it at my disposal, so that I may eat my fill at it as often as I wish.

In your fidelity and goodness grant that I may slake my thirst from this marvelous and intoxicating cup of yours and that, forgetful of my emptiness and wretchedness, my spirit may yearn for you and my soul may burn with love of you.

Hear me, my God, hear me, light of my eyes, hear what I ask, and grant that I may ask what you can give. Faithful God, who are moved by our entreaties, do not fail to be moved because of my sins; rather accept the prayers of your servant because you are good, and grant me what I ask and desire, through the prayers and merits of the glorious Virgin Mary, my Lady, and of all the saints. Amen.

37

Prayer of Desire for Christ[141]

ord Jesus, faithful Jesus, good Jesus, who stooped to die for our sins and who rose for our justification, I ask you by the power of your glorious resurrection to raise me to life from the tomb of all my vices and sins and to grant me a daily participation in the first resurrection, so that I may justly deserve to share in your resurrection.

Most sweet, kind, loving, dear, precious, desirable, lovable, and beautiful Lord, you ascended into heaven in glorious triumph and are now seated at the right hand of the Father.

Most powerful King, draw me after you; I shall run after you in the fragrance of your ointments, I shall run and not grow weary, as you lead and draw me and I run.

Draw the mouth of my soul, which is thirsty for you, to the heavenly streams that slake thirst for ever; yes, draw me to yourself, the living fountain, so that, my God and my life, I may drink from it as much as I can and thereby live forever. For you spoke from your holy and blessed lips and said: *Let anyone who thirsts come to me and drink* (Jn 7:37).

O fountain of life, grant that my thirsting soul may always drink from you, so that in accordance with your holy and truthful promise living waters may stream from my breast![142]

O fountain of life, fill my spirit with the torrent of your delight and intoxicate my heart with the sober drunkenness of your love, so that I may forget the empty things of earth and have you alone constantly in my memory, as it is written: *I remembered God and was delighted* (Ps 76:4)!

Give me your Holy Spirit, symbolized by those waters which you promised to the thirsty.

Grant, I beseech you, that I may aspire with all my desire and all my energy to that place to which we believe you ascended on the fortieth day after your resurrection. Then I shall live on in this wretched state only in body, but shall always be with you in thought and desire. Then my heart will be where you are, my treasure who are so desirable, incomparable, and most lovable.

For on the great flood of this life, on which we are driven by storms that blow from every side, there is no safe anchorage, no place rising out of the waves where the dove's foot can rest. No secure peace, no safe tranquillity; on every side wars and quarrels, on every side enemies; battles without, fears within.

And because one part of us belongs to heaven and the other to earth, the corruptible body weighs down the soul. This is why my spirit, which is my companion and my friend, comes wearied from the journey and languishes and lies prostrate; it is rent and torn by passing vanities, and is intensely hungry and thirsty. I have no bread to set before it, for I am a poor beggar.

Lord my God, you are rich in every good and you are a generous giver of the heavenly food that satisfies; do you, therefore, give food to the wearied, gather what is scattered, and restore to wholeness what has been rent apart.

See, my spirit stands at the door and knocks; I beg you, in the name of the mercy that made you visit us by being born from on high: open the door with a welcoming hand to this poor wretched soul that knocks, and in your mercy bid it enter in to you and rest in you and find refreshment in you, the living bread of heaven, so that when it has been filled it may with renewed strength make its ascent to the heights and, caught up from this valley of tears on the wings of holy desire, it may soar to heavenly joys.

Let my soul, O Lord, take wing like the eagle; let it fly and not be wearied. Let it fly and reach the beauty of your house and the place where your glory dwells. There, at the table at which the citizens of heaven are refreshed, it will feed on your mysteries in your pasture, beside abundant waters.

My God, in you let my heart find rest, this heart that is a great sea of raging waves. You *commanded the winds and the sea, and there came a great calm* (Mt 8:26); come now and walk upon the waves of my heart, that everything in me may become calm and serene. Then I shall embrace you as my sole good, and I shall contemplate you, the sweet light of my eyes, without the blinding darkness of my tumultuous thoughts.

Lord, let my soul flee from the fires of this-worldly thoughts and take refuge under the shadow of your wings; there, hidden in your refreshing coolness, let it sing for joy and say: *In peace in the selfsame I will sleep and rest* (Ps 4:9).

Let my memory be asleep, my God, I pray you, let it be asleep to everything of this world, and let it keep watch in you, as it is written: *I sleep, and my heart keeps watch* (Sg 5:2).

My God, let my soul be safe, let it always be secure, under your protecting wings. Let it remain always in you, and may you always refresh it. Let it contemplate you in ecstasy and sing your praises with jubilation. Amid the whirligig of time let these sweet gifts of yours be my consolation for the interim, until I come to you, my true peace, where there is no bow or shield, no sword or war, but only supreme and certain safety, secure tranquillity and tranquil security, delight-filled happiness, happy eternity, eternal blessedness, and the blessed vision and praise of you for endless ages. Amen.

Lord Christ,[143] power and wisdom of the Father, *who make the clouds your chariot and walk upon the wings of the wind, who make your angels spirits and your ministers a burning fire* (Ps 104:3-4), I beg and beseech you: give me the soaring wings of faith and the swift wings of the virtues so that I can be lifted up and contemplate things eternal and heavenly. Let my soul cling close to you and let your right hand receive me (Ps 62:9). Let that hand raise me above the heights of earth and feed me with the heavenly inheritance for which I yearn night and day in my exile. And since dying members weaken the soul's vigor, dispel the darkness of our earthbound inertia. Make firm my mind that rushes along many straying paths, and grant that it may rise to its heavenly dwelling.[144] Then, illumined by light from on high, it will scorn earth and fix its gaze on heaven, hate sin and love justice. For amid the darkness and bitterness of this present life, what could be more beautiful, what could be sweeter, than to long for the divine sweetness and sigh for everlasting happiness and to have the spirit dwell where true joy is assured?

Most sweet, kind, loving, dear, precious, desirable, lovable, and beautiful Lord, when am I to see you? When shall I appear before your face? When shall my hunger for your beauty be satisfied? When will you lead me out of this dark prison, in order that I may confess your name and thenceforth be afflicted no longer? When shall I enter into that wonderful and beautiful house of yours where *the voice of rejoicing* and gladness echoes *in the tabernacles of the just* (Ps 118:15)?

Blessed are they who dwell in your house; they shall praise you forever and ever (Ps 84:5). Happy, truly happy, are those whom you have already chosen and brought into that heavenly inheritance. See, Lord, your saints flower in your presence like lilies! For they are filled *with the plenty of your house, and you give them drink from the torrent of your pleasure* (Ps 36:9). For you are the fountain of life and in

112

your light they see light, until they, like lights illumined by you, my God, who are the illumining Light, shine like the sun in your sight.

How wonderful, how beautiful, how desirable are the dwelling places of your house!

Lord of powers, this sinful soul of mine desires to enter them. *O Lord, I love the beauty of your house and the place where your glory dwells* (Ps 26:8). *One thing I ask* of you, *this will I seek after: to dwell in* your *house all the days of my life* (Ps 27:4).

As the deer longs for springs of water, so my soul longs for you, my God (Ps 42:2). When shall I come, when shall I appear, when shall I see my God, for whom my soul thirsts? When shall I see him in the land of the living? Here on earth the mortal eyes of the dying cannot see him.

What, then, am I to do, who am a wretch weighed down by the bonds of my mortality? What am I to do? *While we are in the body, we are absent from the Lord* (2 Cor 5:6). *We have not here a lasting city, but we seek one that is to come* (Heb 13:14), for our citizenship is in heaven. *Woe is me, that my sojourning is prolonged! I have dwelt with the inhabitants of Kedar; my soul has been long a sojourner* (Ps 120:5-6). *Who will give me wings like a dove, that I may fly away and be at rest?* (Ps 55:7). Nothing is as sweet for me as to be with my Lord; *it is good for me to be with* my God (Ps 73:28).

Grant, then, O Lord, that as long as I am in this weak body, I may be united to you, for, as it is written, *whoever is joined to the Lord is one spirit* with him (1 Cor 6:17).

Give me, I ask, the wings of contemplation, so that on them I may fly up to you. And since all evil is located here below, keep my soul from falling back into the depths of the dark valley, where the shadows of earth may cover it and separate it from you, the true Sun of Justice, and where dark clouds may keep it from fixing its gaze on high. This is why I strain upward to that delightful and serene state of peace, joy, and light.

Hold my heart in your hand, for without you it cannot be carried up to the heights. I am hastening to the place where supreme peace reigns and continual tranquillity shines brightly. Hold and direct my spirit and conform it to your will, so that with you as its guide it may ascend to that land of abundance where you feed Israel with the food of eternal truth. There, with the utmost rapidity of thought it will reach you, the supreme wisdom that abides above all things and knows all and governs all.

But many things assault the ears of my soul with their noise as it takes flight to you; at your command, Lord, let all things fall silent for me. Let my soul itself fall silent and pass beyond all created things; let it pass beyond even itself and come to you and fix its eyes of faith on you alone, the Creator of all things. Let it yearn for you, strive toward you, meditate on you, contemplate you, set you before its eyes, and in its heart cradle you, who are the true and supreme good and the joy that shall remain forever.

"Many are the forms of contemplation by which the fervent soul is wonderfully fed, but in none of them does the soul find such rest and delight as when it reflects and contemplates in solitude. *O how great is the abundance of your sweetness, Lord* (Ps 31:20), and how wonderfully you inspire the hearts of those who love you!"[145] How marvelously delightful is the love of you which they enjoy who love and seek nothing but you and who even desire to think of naught but you!

Happy they whose only hope is in you and whose only work is prayer!

Blessed they who sit in solitude and silence and faithfully keep watch night and day, in order that while still in this fragile little body they may have some foretaste of your sweetness!

By the saving wounds which you suffered on the cross for our salvation and from which flowed the precious blood of our redemption, wound this sinful soul of mine for which you were willing even to die; wound it with the fiery and powerful dart of your charity that is beyond compare.

You are the living Word of God, *effectual and more piercing than any two-edged sword* (Heb 4:12). You are the choice arrow and sharpest of swords, so powerful that you can penetrate the tough shield of the human heart: pierce my heart, then, with the dart of your love, so that that my soul may say, "I have been wounded by your love,"[146] and abundant tears may flow day and night from this wound of your rich love.

Strike, Lord, strike this hard heart of mine with the sharp spear of your love and by your power pierce deep into my inmost self.

Grant me an abundant source of water and make my eyes a real fountain of ever-flowing tears that spring from a great longing and desire for the vision of your beauty. Then I shall accept no consolations of this present life but shall weep day and night until I am able to see you, my God and my Lord, my beloved and beautiful spouse, in your heavenly chamber. When I see your glorious and wonderful and beautiful and most sweet face, then, with your chosen ones, I shall humbly adore your majesty and, filled at last with the ineffable heavenly joy of everlasting jubilation, I shall cry out with those who love you:

"Now I see what I longed to see; now I possess what I hoped to possess; now I have what I yearned to have! I am united now in heaven to him whom, when I was on earth, I loved with all my strength and embraced with all my love. I cleaved to him with all my heart; now I praise, bless, and adore him who lives and reigns as God for endless ages. Amen."[147]

38

Prayer in Time of Trial[148]

ave mercy on me, O faithful Lord, have mercy on me, a wretched sinner who has acted wrongly and now suffers as he deserves, who has sinned continually and daily suffers your scourges. If I weigh the evil I have done, I do not suffer greatly; my deeds were serious, my burden now is light in comparison.

You are just, O Lord, and your judgment is true; all your judgments are just and true.

You are just and upright, O Lord our God, and there is no evil in you. For neither unjustly nor cruelly do you afflict us sinners, omnipotent and merciful Lord. "When we did not exist, you exerted your power to create us; and when we were lost by our own sin, you brought us back to yourself in a wonderful way."[149]

I know and am certain that chance does not determine our life and that you, the Lord God, direct and govern it. You are solicitous for all, but especially for your servants who have placed all their hope in your mercy alone. Therefore I pray and humbly ask you not to deal with me according to my sins, which have deserved your anger, but according to your own great mercy which is greater than all the sins of the world.

Lord, you inflict these external punishments: grant me also an interior and never-failing patience, so that my mouth may never cease to praise you. Have mercy on me, Lord, have mercy on me and help me as you know I need

116

to be helped in both body and soul. You know everything, you can do everything, and you live forever.

39

Prayer to God the Father for Forgiveness[150]

ord Jesus Christ, Son of the living God, who drank the cup of suffering to its dregs when you spread out your arms on the cross, come to my aid this day.

"See, I come in my poverty to you who are rich, a wretch to you who are merciful; let me not go away empty or spurned. I begin to seek you as one who is hungry; leave me not still in my hunger. I come to you starving; let me not depart unfed. And if I lament before eating, at least let me eat after my lamentation."[151]

First of all, sweet Jesus, in the presence of your magnificent clemency I confess my wickedness. "See, Lord, I was conceived and born in sin, and you washed and sanctified me; yet I afterwards befouled myself with still greater sins. I was born in unavoidable sin; later I wallowed in sins freely chosen."[152]

Yet you, Lord, did not forget to be merciful but removed me from the home of my fleshly father and from the tents of sinners; you inspired me to follow you in the company of the generation that seeks your face: that walks in the straight path, dwells among the lilies of purity, and reclines with you at the supper of deepest poverty.

Yet so ungrateful have I been for these many blessings that after entering religious life I committed many sins and perpetrated many wrongs, and in the place where I should have corrected my faults I added more sins to my old sins. Such are the misdeeds, Lord, by which I have dishonored you and befouled the self which you created in your image and likeness.[153]

Pride, boasting, and many other sins have injured and afflicted, torn and ruined my unhappy soul.

See, Lord, how *my iniquities have risen over my head and like a heavy burden have weighed me down* (Ps 38:5). If you, whose nature it is to have mercy and always to spare, do not support me with the right hand of your majesty, I will be forced to perish wretchedly in the abyss.

Hear me, Lord God, and see, for you are holy: my enemy attacks me, saying: *God has forsaken him; I shall pursue and capture him, for there is no one to deliver him* (Ps 71:11). *But you, O Lord, how long? Turn to me and deliver my soul; save me for your mercy's sake* (Ps 6:4-5). Have mercy on this son of yours, whom you bore with no little pain; do not look at the evil I have done, while forgetting your own goodness. What father is there who will not rescue his son? Or what son is there whose father does not correct him with the rod of tender love?

Father and Lord, even though I am a sinner, I cannot but be your son, for you made me and then made me anew. Since I have sinned, chastise me, and after I have been corrected with your scourge hand me over to your Son. *A mother cannot forget the child of her womb, can she? Yet even if she should forget*, you have promised, Father, that you will not forget (Is 49:15). Yet, see, I cry out and you do not hear me; I am tormented by pain and you do not comfort me!

What then shall I say in my wretchedness or what shall I do? I am so stripped of comfort, I have been cast away from your sight.[154] Alas! From what a great good and into what evil state have I fallen! Where was I going, and whither in fact have I come? Where am I, and where am I not that I should be? To what state did I aspire, and in what state do I now sigh? I sought what was good, and see my trouble now. I am even now dying, but Jesus is not with me. It is indeed better for me not to be than to be without Jesus; better not to live than to live without true life.

And you, Lord Jesus, *where are your ancient mercies?* (Ps 89:50). *Will you be angry with me forever?* (Ps 84:6). Be appeased, I beg you, and have pity on me; *do not turn your face away from me* (Ps 27:9), for in order to redeem me you did not turn your face from those who reproached you and spat at you. I acknowledge that I have sinned; "my conscience merits condemnation, and my penance is not enough to atone; but I believe that your mercy is greater than any offense."[155]

Faithful and loving Lord, do not hold my bitter sayings against me,[156] and *enter not into judgment with your servant* (Ps 143:2); rather, *in accordance with your multitudinous mercies blot out my iniquity* (Ps 50:3).

Woe is me, a wretch, when the day of judgment comes and when the book of each conscience is opened and they say of me: "See the man and his deeds!"

Lord my God, what shall I do then, when the heavens reveal my iniquity and earth rises up against me? I will have no answer to give; I shall hang my head before you in shame and stand there trembling and inarticulate.

Alas, poor wretch! What shall I say? I shall cry out to you, Lord my God. Why should I be eaten up in silence? True, if I speak, my torment will not be appeased; but if I remain silent, I shall be tormented interiorly by an even greater bitterness.

Weep, my soul, like a widow weeping over the husband of her youth; moan and weep, pitiable soul, for your spouse, Christ, has rejected you.

"Wrath of the Almighty, do not fall upon me, for I could never withstand you. There is nothing anywhere in me that could support you."[157] Have pity on me, so that I may not despair but may live on in hope. "I may have done that for which you can condemn me, but you have not lost your power to save."[158] Lord, you do not will the death of sinners,[159] nor do you rejoice when dying persons are lost; on the contrary: you died in order that the dead might live, and your death put the death of sinners to death. If, then, they lived through your death, I beg you, Lord, not to let me die while you live.

Extend your hand from the heights and deliver me from the hand of my enemies; let them not exult over me, *neither let them say: We have swallowed him up* (Ps 35:25).

Good Jesus, who has ever despaired of your mercy? For when we were your enemies you redeemed us with your blood and reconciled us to God.[160] Therefore, protected by your overshadowing mercy, I run to the throne of glory to ask for pardon; I cry out and knock until you take pity on me. For if you called us to forgiveness when we were not seeking forgiveness, how much more surely shall we obtain mercy when we ask for it?

"Most sweet Jesus, do not remember to be just toward this sinner of yours, but be mindful of your kindness toward your creature. Do not remember your anger against one who is guilty, but be mindful of your mercy to the wretched."[161] "Pay no heed to the proud man who provokes you, but look on the unfortunate who invokes you. For what is Jesus, if not a 'Savior'? Therefore, Jesus, come willingly to my aid,"[162] and *say to my soul: I am your salvation* (Ps 34:3). Lord, I expect much from your mercy, because you yourself teach us to ask and seek and knock;[163] at your own invitation, then, "I ask and seek and knock. And do you, Lord, who bid me ask, see to it that I receive; you advise me to seek, grant that I may find; you teach me to knock, open to me when I do knock."[164]

Strengthen me who am weak, restore me who am lost, raise me up who am dead. Deign to direct and govern all my senses and thoughts and actions according to your will, so that henceforth I may serve you and live for you and may surrender myself to you.

My Lord, I know that because you made me, I owe my whole being to you; and because you redeemed me and became a human being for me, I owe you even more than myself if that were possible, for you are greater than this poor wretch for whom you gave yourself. I have no more to give, and even what I have I cannot give to you without your help; receive me, then, and draw me to yourself, so that I may be yours in love and imitation, just as I belong by my nature to you who live and reign forever.

40

Prayer in Remembrance of the Passion of Christ[165]

ord, almighty God, who are Three and One, you are always in all and were before all and will always be in all: God blessed through endless ages! I commend to your mighty hands, today and always, my soul and body, my sight and hearing, my taste and smell and touch, all my thoughts and sufferings, my words and actions, everything external to me and interior to me: senses and intellect and memory, persevering faith and belief, so that you may guard them night and day, at every hour and every moment.

Hear me, O holy Trinity, and protect me against all evil, all scandal, all serious sin, all snares and onslaughts of demons and of enemies visible and invisible. Protect me through the prayers of the patriarchs, the merits of the prophets, the intercession of the apostles, the constancy of the martyrs, the faith of confessors, the chastity of virgins, and the intercession of all the saints who have pleased you since the beginning of the world.

Rid me of any boastful spirit and intensify my compunction of heart; lessen my pride and bring me to true humility; start the fountain of tears in me and soften my hard and stony heart.

Deliver me and deliver my soul, O Lord, from all the snares of the enemy, and preserve me in your will. Lord, *teach me to do your will, for you are my God* (Ps 143:10).

"Grant me, Lord, perfection of heart and understanding that I may be able to grasp the depths of your kindness. Grant that I may ask what you love to hear and what is of profit to me. Grant me heartfelt tears that can loosen the bonds of my sins. Hear, my Lord and my God, hear what I ask, and teach me to ask for what you can grant. If you scorn me, I am lost; if you gaze on me with favor, I come to life; if you look for justice in me, I am a corrupt dead man; if you look on me with mercy, you raise the corrupt one from the tomb. Put far from me what you detest in me."[166]

Let the spirit of continence and chastity take root in me, so that there may be nothing to offend you in any petition I offer to you. Take from me what is harmful and grant me what will profit me.

Bestow on me, O Lord, a medicine to heal my wounds. Grant me fear of you, compunction of heart, humility of spirit, and a pure conscience. Give me strength always to observe fraternal charity; let me not forget the evil I have done and go looking for evil in others. Spare my soul, spare it despite its evils and sins and wickedness. Visit me in my weakness, heal me of my sickness, cure me of my languor, and raise me from my death.

"Grant me, Lord, a heart that fears you, a soul that loves you, a mind that understands you, ears that hear you, eyes that see you."[167] Have pity on me, Lord, have pity on me; look favorably on me from your throne of majesty and shed light into the darkness of my heart with the rays of your splendor.

Grant me discernment to distinguish between good and evil, and a watchful mind. I ask you, Lord, for the forgiveness of all my sins, for it is from and through you that mercy is shown me in time of need and affliction.

Mary, holy and spotless, Virgin Mother of God and Mother of our Lord Jesus Christ, intercede for me with him whose temple you were judged worthy to become. Michael, Gabriel, Raphael, holy choirs of angels and archangels, of patriarchs and prophets, of apostles, evangelists, martyrs, confessors, priests, levites, monks, virgins, and all the just: in the name of him who chose you and whom it is your delight to contemplate, I make bold to ask you to pray to God for me in my guilt, that I be rescued from the jaws of the devil and from everlasting death. Lord, deign to bestow eternal life on me in accordance with your clemency and merciful kindness.

Lord Jesus Christ, grant harmony among priests and tranquillity and peace to kings, bishops, and princes who judge justly. I pray, Lord, for the entire holy Catholic Church, for men and women, religious and laity, all Christian rulers, and all believers in you who toil out of holy love for you, that they may persevere in good deeds.

Lord, eternal King, grant chastity to virgins, continence to those consecrated to God, fidelity to spouses, indulgence to penitents, assistance to widows and orphans, protection to the poor, a return home to pilgrims,[168] comfort to the afflicted, eternal rest to the faithful departed, and a safe port to travelers at sea.

"Grant that the good may always remain good, that the mediocre may become better, and that the wicked and offenders may quickly change their ways."[169]

O most sweet and merciful Lord Jesus Christ, Son of the living God and Redeemer of the world, I confess that of all human beings I am in all things a wretched sinner. But, most merciful and supreme Father, who have pity on all, do not allow me to be separated from your mercy.

Lord, King of kings, who determine how long we are to live, grant me devotion so that I may correct my ways. Inspire in me a spirit that seeks and desires you, a spirit that always and in all things loves and fears you who are everywhere Three and One and that does your will.

Above all, Lord, holy Father, who are blessed and glorious through all ages, I pray for all those who remember me in their prayers or have commended themselves to my unworthy prayers or have made some charitable gesture or pious effort on my behalf or who are bound to me by any bond of blood or relationship, be they still in the body or already hidden from us by death, that you would in your mercy guide them so that they do not perish.

Bestow your help on all living Christians and absolution and eternal rest through all ages on the faithful departed. I also urgently implore you, Lord, who are the alpha and the omega, that when my last day and the end of my life comes, you yourself will be my merciful judge against the devil with his malicious accusations and my perpetual defender against the attacks of the ancient enemy.

Grant that I may have a permanent place in your holy paradise and in the company of the angels and all the saints. This is my prayer to you who are blessed through endless ages. Amen.

41

Meditation on the Passion and Resurrection of Christ[170]

ord Jesus Christ, my redemption, my mercy, my salvation, I praise you, I give you thanks. Although my praises fall far short of your blessings and are so lacking in true devotion, although they are so insubstantial in comparison with the utterly desirable richness of your sweet love, yet my soul does offer you its praises and thanks — not such as I realize are due to you, but such as I can try to give.

Hope of my heart, strength of my soul, help in my weakness, let your all-powerful kindness accomplish what my weakness and tepidity can only attempt. My life and the goal of my striving consist in loving you; indeed my merits fall short of my debt to you, but at least I desire to love you as you deserve.

Lord, my light, you see my conscience, for *all my desire is before you* (Ps 38:10) and any good desire I have is your doing. Lord, if what you inspire in me is good, and since it is good for me to love you, grant me that which you cause me to desire: grant that I may love you as much as you bid me love you.

I praise and thank you for the desire which you have aroused in me. I praise you and pray that the gift which you have freely given me may not remain fruitless. Complete what you have begun; give me what your prevenient kindness has caused me to desire.

Most merciful one, the goal of my prayer, the goal of my remembrance and meditation on your gifts, is that I might fan in myself the flame of love of you. Lord, it was your goodness that created me, your mercy that cleansed me from original sin after you had created me, your patience that has put up with me and fed me and waited for me when after the cleansing of baptism I rolled in the mire of other sins.

Lord, in your goodness you look for me to change my ways; my soul in turn looks to the inspiration of your grace that it may adequately repent and live a good life.

My God, my Creator, you have put up with me and fed me; be my helper now. I thirst for you, I hunger for you, I want you, I sigh for you, I ardently desire you. As an orphan, deprived of the presence of its kindly father, constantly embraces that beloved face with all its heart amid weeping and lamentation, so do I weep, not as I ought but as I can, when I recall your suffering, the blows you bore, your scourging and cross and wounds, when I recall how you suffered for me, how you were hidden away and buried, and when I remember, too, your glorious resurrection and wonderful ascension. All these I believe in with unhesitating faith, as I lament the trials of my exile and hope for your coming, which is my only comfort, and ardently desire to see your glorious face.

Alas, I was not able to see the Lord of the angels when he humbled himself to live among human beings in order that he might lift them up to live with the angels! and when, though he was the offended God, he died that sinners might live!

Alas, I did not deserve to be present and astounded by such wonderful, inestimable love!

Why, O my soul, have you not at least been pierced by the sword of profound repentance, since you were not able to see the side of your Savior wounded by the lance, the hands and feet of your Maker torn by the nails, and the blood of your Redeemer poured out! Why are you not made drunk on bitter tears when he had to drink bitter gall?

Why have you not suffered with the chaste Virgin, his most worthy Mother and your kindly Lady?

My most merciful Lady, how shall I describe the flood of tears that poured from your modest eyes when you saw your only Son, despite his innocence, being bound and scourged and sacrificed before your eyes?

What tears covered your loving face when you looked up to see your God and Lord, though innocent, extended on the cross and this flesh of your flesh so cruelly torn by the wicked?

What sobs must have racked your pure breast when you heard addressed to you the words: *Woman, this is your son,* and to the disciple: *This is your mother* (Jn 19:26-27), and you received a disciple in place of the Teacher, a servant in place of the Lord?

Would that I had joined happy Joseph in taking my Lord down from the cross and embalming him with perfumes and laying him in the tomb, or that I had at least gone before or followed after, thus offering my little service for the funeral!

Would that with the blessed women I had been terrified by the bright vision of angels and heard the message of the Lord's resurrection, a message so consoling to me, a message so awaited and so desired!

Would that I had heard from the angel's lips: *Be not afraid! You seek Jesus who was crucified; he is risen, he is not here* (Mk 16:6)!

Kind, sweet, tranquil Lord, when will you bring all this home to me, since I did not see your blessed flesh now incorrupt or kiss the place of the wounds, the marks of the nails, or sprinkle with tears of joy the scars that proved your body to be real?

O marvelous, unimaginable, incomparable Lord, when will you console me and release me from my pain? For my suffering is beyond measure as long as I am in exile from my Lord.

Alas, how unhappy is my soul! You, the consolation of my life, went away and did not bid me farewell. As you went your way you blessed your disciples, but I was not there; with hands raised you were carried up to heaven on a cloud,[171] but I did not see it; the angels promised that you would return, but I did not hear it.

What am I to say or do? Where am I to seek him? Where or when shall I find him? Whom shall I ask? Who will tell the beloved that *I languish with love* (Sg 2:5)? The joy of my heart has faded, my laughter has turned into mourning; my flesh and my heart have fainted away,

O God of my heart, God who are my portion for eternity! My soul has refused to be consoled by anything but you, my sweetness. *For what have I in heaven, and besides you what do I desire upon earth?* (Ps 73:25). I want you, I hope for you, I seek you. *My heart said to you: I have sought your face; your face, O Lord, I will seek; turn not your face from me* (Ps 28:8-9).

Most kind lover of humanity, the poor have abandoned themselves to you; you will help the orphaned. My advocate and secure shelter, have pity on this abandoned orphan; I have become an orphan without a father; my soul is like a widow. Look on the tears of one thus orphaned and widowed, for I offer them to you until you return.

Lord, show yourself to me and I shall be consoled; show me your face and I shall be saved. Make your presence known to me, and I shall obtain what I desire; reveal your glory to me, and my joy shall be complete. *My soul has thirsted for you, for you my flesh, in how many ways!* (Ps 63:2). *My soul has thirsted for God, the living fountain; when*

shall I come and appear before the face of my God? (Ps 42:3).
When will you come, my Consoler whom I await?

If only I may one day see my joy, whom I desire! If only
I may be satisfied when your glory appears,[172] for which I
hunger! If only I may be inebriated by the abundance of
your house, for which I long! If only you will give me to
drink from the torrent of your pleasure,[173] for which I
thirst! Meanwhile, Lord, let my tears be my bread day and
night, until they say to me: "This is your Lord!"[174] and I
hear the words: "Soul, here is your spouse!" Until then,
nourish me with my sobs, give me my tears to drink, comfort me with my sorrows. Meanwhile, perhaps my Redeemer will come, for he is good; he will not delay, for he
is faithful. To him be glory through endless ages. Amen.

Notes

The Latin text of the *Meditations* is in *Patrologia Latina* (henceforth: PL) 40,901-942.

1. This entire first chapter is the beginning of Saint Anselm's *Prayers* 10: PL 158, 877-878.

2. This entire chapter is a continuation of Saint Anselm's *Prayers* 10: PL 158, 878-880.

3. See Ps 18:3.

4. See Lk 11:2.

5. See Ps 51:19.

6. See Lk 8:13.

7. See Ps 140:8.

8. "Tribulation" (*tribulatio*) sums up all the trials and troubles, especially spiritual, that threaten Christians during their earthly lives. The phrase "great tribulation" is sometimes used of the catastrophes at the end of time.

9. The entire third chapter is, once again, from Saint Anselm's *Prayers* 10; continuation of the preceding two chapters, PL 158, 180-181.

10. See Ps 27:1.

11. This paragraph has been using the image of a military action, traditional in speaking of the spiritual struggle (see Saint Paul). The image has its logical extension in the idea of wounds and sickness, which are two words for sin.

12. See Prv 26:11.

13. See 2 Pt 2:22.

14. We hear in this passage the confession of a pastor of souls, one responsible for the people entrusted to his care (a man such as

Saint Anselm, who was initially the abbot of Bec-Hellouin and then Archbishop of Canterbury).

15. In Isaiah God is compared to a woman in labor; after a long silence during which he has been patient, he finally manifests his power to human beings. Since the text was part of the Divine Office, Saint Anselm was obviously familiar with the image.

16. Continuation of Saint Anselm's *Prayers* 10: PL 158, 881-883.

17. See Ps 50:3-4.

18. Readers may be surprised to see a reference to monastic life following this list of sins. There is no way for us to get inside the consciousness of the author.

19. In the psalms a "holy man" is one who lives in a proper relation to God (such persons as Moses and King David). "Kedar" is the name of an (Ishmaelite) tribe that has a rather poor reputation throughout the Bible; to dwell in Kedar means to be far from God and his help.

20. This and the following chapters are from the second of Saint Anselm's *Prayers:* PL 158, 858-865.

21. See Ps 145:18.

22. This paragraph is a good example of the way the author plays on words. Here the formula "to call upon the Truth in truth" gives rise to a meditation on truth. The exercise may strike us as rather unprofitable, but if we look at it more closely, it can have its spiritual usefulness. We should keep in mind that, following Saint Augustine, the spiritual writers of the medieval period had a great devotion to the letter of the scriptures; this partly explains their close attention to words.

23. See Jn 1:1.

24. After the play on "truth" there is a play on the Latin *principium* with its two meanings of "source" and "beginning." "Word," moreover, can mean speech, or words (such as Saint Anselm looks for in his prayer), or the Word par excellence that expresses God and that for our sake became a human being.

25. See Rom 8:34.

26. See Is 53:7.

27. See 1 Pt 2:22.24.

28. Saint Anselm, *Prayers* 2: PL 158, 860-861.

29. See Mt 3:17.

30. See Is 53:9.12.

31. This meditation is on Saint Anselm's conception of "vicarious satisfaction": the God-man makes satisfaction to divine justice by his obedience unto death. The middle ages will accept and follow this view, though with nuances and reservations.

32. These lines reflect the economy or plan of salvation in which the sacrifice of Christ is linked to original sin (the tree of the cross is an echo as it were of the tree with the forbidden fruit) and in which there is a parallelism between the two Adams and the two Eves (a conception that is very ancient: Saint Paul, Saint Justin, Saint Irenaeus).

33. See Gal 5:24.

34. This passage explains why the meditations of Saint Anselm are so often filled with sorrow and tears: through repentance our suffering for our sins can be united to the suffering of Christ, which was due to these very sins; even our sins thus provide a way of redemption through love of Christ.

35. See Ps 42:4.

36. See Ps 119:72.

37. Saint Anselm, *Prayers* 2: PL 158, 863-865.

38. See Lk 15:4-7. According to the Fathers of the Church, the lost sheep is the whole human race that had distanced itself from God (Gregory of Nyssa, Augustine). The theme was also rendered familiar through Christian art.

39. "Justice versus injustice" is a frequent theme in these meditations. Concretely understood, justice means being just (like Christ, the only Just One), or justified (that is, saved, rendered just, by Christ). Injustice means being unjust, that is, departing from the will of God and incurring rejection.

40. Impiety consists in not giving God what is due to him. Piety, for its part, means more than simply fervor or devotion; it consists above all in doing all that God expects of us. Thus the culmination of the Son's piety is his sacrifice on the cross, which was a sacrifice of praise consisting in perfect obedience to the Father's will. It is in

this full sense that "piety" is usually to be understood in the *Meditations*.

41. Since the Lord's goodness will always be greater than human sin, each sin will as it were only increase God's mercy. Something of this idea is reflected in the traditional formulas: *Where sin abounded, grace abounded all the more* (Rom 5:20); and "O happy fault, that gained for us so great a Redeemer!" (Easter Proclamation).

42. This entire chapter is from Saint Anselm's *Prayers* 14: PL 158, 888.

43. See Ps 36:9.

44. See Jn 14:25.

45. See Ps 9:10.

46. This entire short chapter is from Saint Anselm's *Prayers* 21; PL 158, 905. The play on worthiness and unworthiness may strike us today as somewhat labored, but it was a meditation device common among the Fathers. See above, Chapter 5, note 22.

47. The author of this homage to the Trinity, in the form of a doxology, is unknown, and the text is not found in all manuscripts. It serves as an introduction to the following chapter on the Trinity.

48. Here begins the first part of John of Fécamp's little work *Booklet (Libellus)*: PL 147, 457. See also his *Theological Confession* I, 14 (ed. J. Leclercq and J.-P. Bonnes, *Un maître de la vie spirituelle au XIe siècle* [Paris, 1946] 119-120); henceforth the page number of this edition will be given in parentheses after references. The *Booklet* is essentially a meditation based on the scriptures and the words of the Fathers. In it we will find various authors cited (the chief ones will be noted) and, in particular, citations from other works of John himself. The style is not very different from that of Saint Anselm, but the tone becomes more joyous and less plaintive, and more directed to praise.

49. The work is thus dedicated to the Trinity. The author now begins a lengthy confession of faith; the spate of descriptive words that follows brings out the incomprehensibility of God.

50. This passage is from the *Mirror (Speculum)* which was for a long time attributed to Saint Augustine (PL 40, 967-989; see Patro-

logiae Latinae Supplementum [henceforth: PLS] 2:1366), but which seems to be in fact from John's own pen (see *Mirror* 24: PL 40, 979). See the Introduction to the present translation.

51. Citation from *Confession of Faith* 2, 1: PL 101, 1047. This work was long attributed to Alcuin, but seems to be the work of John himself. See especially *Theological Confession* II, 1, 2, 3 (page 121). The emphasis on the Trinity and Christ's place in it is due to the importance which the whole of medieval Christology assigned to the conciliar definitions against heresies that were still regarded as a threat.

52. See Col 2:14.

53. See Jn 10:18.

54. This paragraph is a quite free citation of Saint Augustine, *Confessions* X, 43, 69.

55. See Rom 8:34.

56. Allusion to Saint Paul and the doctrine of the Church as a body whose head is Christ.

57. Free citation of John's *Confession of Faith* 2, 5. See also his *Theological Confession* II, 6.

58. Free citation of *Confession of Faith* 4, 11. The same citation recurs below in chapter 38.

59. See the Preface for Pentecost in the pre-Vatican II Missal.

60. An echo of *Theological Confession* II, 6 (page 128).

61. See Lk 15:4-5.

62. See Rom 8:3-4.

63. Easter Preface (pre-Vatican II Missal); Easter Preface I (Vatican II Missal).

64. See Heb 2:16.

65. Those who regard this exaltation of humanity above the angels as excessively bold should recall that it expresses the Pauline teaching found in the Captivity Letters, especially Col 2:6-23. In any case, it bears witness to an immense hope.

66. According to Saint Paul (Eph 5), husband is united to wife as Christ is to the Church. The marriage theme, inherited from the Old Testament and a familiar one in the gospels and the Pauline letters, is a way of expressing the union of Christ and the Church.

It is developed by the entire patristic tradition, for example, Origen, Gregory of Elvira, Hilary of Poitiers.

67. See Rom 4:25.

68. See Rom 8:34.

69. See Jn 5:22.

70. See Rom 8:17.

71. See John of Fécamp, *Theological Confession* II, 3, 5, 6.

72. John of Fécamp, *Confession of Faith* 2, 6; 14, 12. See *Theological Confession* II, 6, 14.

73. *Confession of Faith* 2, 7 (free citation).

74. See Prv 39:4.

75. *Ibid.*, 2, 10 (free citation). The final sequence of phrases ("supreme and sure security," etc.) exemplifies a stylistic device much cultivated by the Fathers and by Augustine in particular: a list in which the noun of one phrase becomes the adjective in the next. See, for example, Saint Augustine, *The Trinity* IV, Prologue 1 (at the end).

76. A hymn that seems to be the work of Gottschalk of Fulda (+869), to whom it is attributed by G. M. Dreves and C. Blume (eds.), *Analecta hymnica Medii Aevi* (55 vols.; Leipzig, 1896-1922) 50:235-236.

77. The reader may be surprised to hear Christ being called "Father." The title is based on his having engendered the Church by his grace (Saint Paul) and is found in Clement of Alexandria, in prayers in the apocryphal *Acts*, and in the *Rule* of Saint Benedict.

78. See Ps 30:21.

79. Saint Augustine, *Confessions* XIII, 8, 9.

80. The "Songs of Ascents" or Gradual Psalms (Psalms 121-135) were sung by pilgrims going up to Jerusalem.

81. Saint Augustine, *Confessions* XII, 16, 17.

82. This meditation on the house of the Lord is inspired by Saint Augustine, *Confessions* XI, 11, 13 to XI, 30, 40, and reminds us of one of Augustine's favorite ideas, the "city of God."

83. Medieval writers are sometimes accused of having had a naive idea of paradise as a geographical place. This passage, however, brings out the spiritual dimension of the heavenly Jerusalem,

which in Chapter 20 is connected with the communion of saints and the idea that "the kingdom of God is in our midst."

84. See Ps 149:6.

85. See Sir 1:4.

86. See Gn 1:1.

87. See 2 Cor 5:21.

88. See Sir 1:4.

89. See Gal 4:26.

90. Saint Augustine, *Confessions* XII, 11, 12-13. For the meaning of "day" see Saint Augustine, *Expositions of the Psalms* 38, 7.

91. Saint Augustine, *Confessions* XII, 15, 21.

92. Another theme dear to Augustine, stated in the *Confessions* IX, 13, 37, and developed at length in the commentaries on the Psalms and especially in *City of God* XIX, 17.

93. When Saint Paul says that the Lord "made one people of the two," he is referring to Israel and the Gentiles, whom Christ has united through the sacrifice that establishes the new covenant. John of Fécamp applies the idea to human beings and angels, who are united by Christ in his glorified flesh.

94. The pilgrimage is the pilgrimage of earthly life, a thought often invoked by Saint Augustine. See his comments on Ps 50:22 and Ps 138:12-13: "Love the other life, and you will see that this one is nothing but tribulation."

95. *Mirror* 30. See *Meditation* 12, note 38.

96. The "deceiver" is earthly life, which seduces human beings by persuading them that it will make them happy, but in the end leads those it deceives into an everlasting death.

97. This lengthy reference to monastic life with its study and its entire "Benedictine work" shows us the meaning of *lectio divina*. See D. Gorce, *La "lectio divina": S. Jérôme et la lecture sacrée* (Paris, 1925).

98. *Mirror* 30 (continuation of the passage cited at note 47).

99. Verse from an unknown author.

100. Saint Gregory the Great, *Homilies on the Gospels* 37, 1: PL 76, 1275).

101. Free citation of *Mirror* 29.

102. It seems odd to find mythological creatures appearing in the midst of biblical images. It must be remembered, however, that Latin culture was the chief vehicle of Christian thought for the medieval writers; it is therefore not surprising that they should make use of the most eloquent images at their disposal. Besides, the two monsters associated with the Strait of Messina are not out of place in the list of marine creatures nor in the image of life as a journey by sea.

103. *Mirror* 30.

104. See Sg 7:12.

105. Hymn at one time attributed to Saint Peter Damian, a contemporary and fellow-countryman of John of Fécamp, and added to the *Meditations* at a later stage but serving as a fine complement to the description of paradise in Chapter 25. Damian's authorship is rejected today. Text in Dreves and Blume (note 76, above) 48:65. See J. A. Hurlbut, *The Song of Saint Peter Damian on the Joys and Glory of Paradise* (Washington, D.C., 1928).

106. The vocabulary of the military life (*palma, post solutum militare cingulum, donativum*, etc.) does not seem very poetic; the image, based on the career of a Roman legionary, is part of the Augustinian tradition, according to which Christians, and especially religious, are soldiers fighting in the service of Christ, who is their reward.

107. Here begins the third part of John of Fécamp's *Confession of Faith*: PL 101, 1053.

108. Saint Gregory the Great, *Homilies on Ezekiel* I, hom. 8, 15: PL 76, 860; a somewhat free citation.

109. This paragraph, which is inspired by Saint Gregory the Great (note 60), occurs again in *Spirit and Soul* (*De spiritu et anima*) (PL 40, 799-832), a work that was for a long time attributed to Augustine but was more probably composed in circles connected with Saint Bernard (see PLS 2,1364-1365). It thus attests to the importance of the *Meditations* in their day, since they served as a source for other writers. See *Spirit and Soul* 56.

110. This short chapter is an introduction to the extended praise offered in Chapter 29; it is like a Preface before a Sanctus.

111. *Mirror* 3, 5: PL 40, 970-971.

112. These first four chapters come from the *Mirror* 4: PL 40, 971. As in Chapter 12, this accumulation of paradoxical statements about the divinity is intended to make readers more aware of the incomprehensible immensity of God.

113. A reference to metaphysics and to Ex 3:14: God is He Who Is, Being (*ôn*) itself. See *Mirror* 30: PL 40, 892.

114. *Mirror* 23 and 24: PL 40, 978-979. Homage is here paid to the Church for teaching us the mystery of the Trinity; during the early centuries of the Church's life heretical views of the Trinity were so numerous that the Fathers always laid great emphasis on this mystery.

115. "Form" is a metaphysical concept that Christian writers used long before the rise of Scholasticism. In summary: every being of our experience is composed of matter and form; without matter, form is simply an abstraction; without form, matter remains indeterminate. God, who is Being par excellence, is also Form par excellence, inasmuch as it is he who gives all things their form. As ideal form, he does not need matter in order to exist; therefore he is not material or corporeal. He is He Who Is. See Chapter 29.

116. *Mirror* 20-22: PL 40, 977-978.

117. *Mirror* 23: PL 40, 978.

118. See note 114, above.

119. These first three chapters are from the *Mirror* 1: PL 40, 967.

120. *ôn* = Being (see note 113, above); see *Mirror* 39: PL 40, 983.

121. Logos = Word.

122. *Mirror* 30: PL 40, 982.

123. The text thus far is from Saint Augustine, *Soliloquies* I, 1, 3.

124. *Mirror* 1: PL 40, 967.

125. Saint Augustine, *Confessions* I, 1, 1. Free citation.

126. Saint Augustine, *Confessions* VII, 10, 16.

127. See 1 Jn 3:2.

128. Saint Anselm, *Prayers:* 1 PL 158:858.

129. This chapter is not by John of Fécamp, but is entirely from Saint Anselm's *Prayers* 5: PL 158:871. It is a contemplative prayer

of the kind which the French of the seventeenth century called "elevations." The style reflects the genre, displaying a great feeling of distress.

130. Here begins the fourth part of John of Fécamp's *Booklet* (PL 147:457). This chapter also provides the material for the entirety of Saint Anselm's *Prayers* 17: PL 158:894; this probably means that the great saint was pleased to use the writings of his illustrious Benedictine brother.

131. Allusion to the parable of the dishonest steward (Lk 16:1-8): *The children of this age are more shrewd in dealing with their own generation than are the children of light* (verse 8).

132. Saint Augustine, *Confessions* X, 29, 40.

133. Here begins the fifth part of John of Fécamp's *Booklet* (PL 147:159). This chapter, along with the preceding, was taken over by Saint Anselm for his *Prayers* 16: PL 158, 891.

134. See Lk 12:49.

135. See 1 Sm 1:18.

136. The gift of tears is here viewed as a strict charism that makes possible a profound conversion and liberation.

137. This paragraph on Mary Magdalene is a paraphrase of Saint Gregory the Great, *Homilies on the Gospel* 25, 2 (PL 76:1179).

138. See Jn 20:11-17.

139. See Jn 11:35.

140. See Lk 19:41.

141. Here begins the sixth part of John's *Booklet* (PL 147:159), which Saint Anselm took over in its entirety in his *Prayers* 18 (PL 158:897-899).

142. See Jn 7:38.

143. Here begins the seventh part of John's *Booklet* (PL 147:160), which Saint Anselm uses in *Prayers* 19 (PL 158:899).

144. Verse from an unidentifiable author; see *Mirror* 3.

145. *Mirror* 33 (PL 40:984); a free citation.

146. This heart pierced by the lance of love anticipates the "transverberation" of the great mystics, for example, Saint Teresa of Jesus of Avila.

147. This is the end of John's *Booklet* on the scriptures and passages from the Fathers.

148. John of Fécamp, *Divine Contemplation* (*De divina contemplatione*), eighth prayer: PL 147,461. This passage from another work of John was added to the *Meditations* by an unknown hand.

149. Free citation of *Confession of Faith* 4, 11 (the same passage was cited earlier in Chapter 14). It is clear that John did not hesitate to cite himself in his various writings.

150. This chapter is a paraphrase of various passages from Saint Anselm's *Proslogion*, *Meditations*, and *Prayers*, with some verbatim summaries.

151. Saint Anselm, *Proslogion* 1 (John cites the original in a disordered fashion).

152. Saint Anselm, *Prayers* 62: PL 158,969.

153. See Gn 1:27.

154. See Ps 31:23.

155. Saint Anselm, *Meditations* 3 (PL 158:729).

156. See Jb 13:26.

157. *Ibid.*, 2 (PL 158:724).

158. *Ibid.*, 3 (PL 158:729). What follows here summarizes and paraphrases Saint Anselm's thought.

159. See Ez 33:11.

160. See Rom 5:10.

161. *Ibid.*, 3 (at end) (PL 158:759).

162. *Ibid.*, 2 (at end) (PL 158:724).

163. See Mt 7:7.

164. *Ibid.*, 11 (at end) (PL 158:769).

165. This chapter would seem to be from John of Fécamp if we may judge by its style, which "smacks of John of Fécamp" (so the Maurists) and by its citations from Alcuin. But there is no certainty on the point, and we do not know the source. In any case, it develops themes already found in preceding chapters, for example, 35. See A. Wilmart, *Auteurs spirituels*, 99-100.

166. Alcuin, *The Sacraments* 1 (PL 101:446) (free citation).

167. Alcuin, from a confession in which he speaks of the sins of which he had become aware by reading a commentary on the Psalms.

168. Allusion to the lengthy pilgrimages undertaken in the middle ages to Santiago de Compostella, Rome, or Jerusalem. These lasted several months or even several years, and the pilgrims were never sure they would return safely; the dangers to pilgrims provided a regular intention in the Church's prayer.

169. Saint Anselm, first prayer to the Trinity (PL 158:855). We do not know whether the formulary was a widespread one which two different authors happened to use, or whether Anselm took it from the text here.

170. Saint Anselm, *Prayers* 20: PL 158:902.

171. See Lk 24:50-51.

172. See Ps 17:15.

173. See Ps 36:9.

174. See Ps 42:4.

Thematic Guide

Theological Implications

The *Meditations* may well be described as theological because the doctrinal points of reference are so firm and clear: God one and triune, the incarnation, the two natures of Christ, the history of salvation, the action of the Spirit, eschatology. These major themes are usually developed over several chapters.

To whom are the *Meditations* addressed?

In fidelity to the liturgy, the author usually addresses his prayer to God, that is, the Father. Several chapters are meditations on the mystery of God (27, 28, 29, 30, 31). A number of prayers are addressed to the Trinity (11, 12, 13, 30, 31) and make us think at times of Elizabeth of the Trinity.

Other prayers are addressed to Christ as mediator (18, 34, 35, 38). A few shift from the Father to the Son or return from Christ to the Father (39). The Holy Spirit is addressed in chapter 9.

The mystery of God

A series of meditations is devoted to God (27-31), his impenetrable mystery (27), and the countless wonders of his perfections, which elicit adoration and praise (31, 32).

The coming and passion of Christ

The plan of salvation, to which reference is often made (7, 14, 17), has its center in the incarnation (13-17). We see here the importance which the middle ages assigned to the passion of the Son (6-8) — which provided an inexhaustible source of meditation, trust, and hope — and to the redemption (17).

Frequent reference is made to the mediation of Christ in the history of salvation. In fact, this mediation is the vital heart of this history. The reader will not miss the passionate tone of affective devotion, which anticipates Bernard (35). Christ is guide for the entire life of believers (5, 8, 14, 15, 16, 40); by Christ is meant chiefly the Christ who has entered into the glory of God (15).

Other themes which make an appearance

There is a reference to the eucharist (6) and several to the Church as spouse and body of Christ (4, 29, 30). The lost sheep represents the entire human race being brought back to the fold.

A School of Prayer

The *Meditations* derive their inspiration from scripture (more so than may appear at first glance), with special preference given to the Song of Songs and above all to the psalms, which are cited in great abundance (see the Index of Biblical Citations). There is a formal reference to *lectio divina*, the reading of scripture (22).

The influence of Augustine can be seen chiefly in the familiarity with the psalms, the prayerbook of the people of God, both old and new. Like Christ himself, the Fathers — Origen, Hilary, Ambrose, Augustine — make the prayers of the psalmists their own (see the Index of Biblical Citations).

The main ideas

One trait typical of these "elevations" is the place given to praise; praise is constant and is present, explicitly or by allusion, in every setting (for example, 26 and 32 but also in the whole series 27-33). Praise sets the tone for the entire book.

Praise usually leads into thanksgiving, especially at the thought of God's saving deeds and of Christ's mediation (14-17, 41).

In the presence of the unfathomable mystery of God those praying might well feel overwhelmed, but faith tells them of the goodness of God (8, 15) and his mercy to sinners (2, 16, 34, 35, 39) and gives rise to an unshakable sense of confidence and self-surrender (4).

Consciousness of sin

The *Meditations* frequently dwell on the sinful human condition. The influence of Augustine's *Confessions* is especially evident here, extending to the ambiguity of the word "confess" itself, which can mean both to confess the mercy of God and to confess human wretchedness and sinfulness.

The thought of the sins of Christians returns like a leitmotiv in many chapters (3, 4, 5, 7, 34, 35, 39). The person praying suffers in conscience (3) and comes before God in a spirit of repentance

(1). He humbles himself in order to obtain mercy (10, 34). Along with the middle ages as a whole, he asks for the gift of tears (36).

The trials of life

Whether as a consequence of sin or due to something inherent in the human condition, human beings are subject to trial and tribulation (38) and to temptations and the attacks of the demon (24). A whole meditation has the wretchedness of human life as its subject (21; see also 3, 33, 36, 37).

The tragic aspect of human existence emerges especially in texts from Saint Anselm (34, 35, 37, 39).

Journey to the House of God

The eschatological perspective is developed at length and in a series of chapters (22-25). In a more diffuse way the quest of God (1, 36, 40, 41) and the longing for beatitude (18-21) occupy a considerable part of the *Meditations* as a whole.

Expectation and its tension also make it possible to sense the gap between time and eternity. This Augustinian theme comes to the fore in chapter 19.

Judgment

Fear of the judge is evoked in chapter 4, although it does not take on the tone of terror which it has in the *Dies irae*. In this context, fear disposes the soul for repentance but also for trust in the goodness of God. It climaxes in a trinitarian doxology.

The house of God

Christians are pilgrims; every prayer is a pilgrimage to the Jerusalem that is on high (21), to the house of God (20), the happiness promised to us (25), and everlasting life (22). One chapter is a hymn that sings of the future paradise (26).

The communion of saints

It is in this evocation of the end and future state that awareness of what the Church is expands to its full form in the doctrine of the communion of saints, which is often invoked (24, 15, 17). The saints are not only God's chosen ones, but also intercessors for the journeying Church at prayer. On several occasions we catch an echo as it were of the *Te Deum* (25, 40).

The place of Mary

The *Meditations* assign an important place to the Virgin Mary, who is mentioned in several settings (7, 36, 40, 41). The most surprising is in the fortieth meditation (which is undoubtedly a late addition): "Holy Mary, Mother of God, spotless Virgin, deign to intercede for me."